3PRACTICES
for Crossing the Difference Divide

Jim Henderson + Jim Hancock

OffTheMap.com

Seattle

© 2019 Jim Henderson and Jim Hancock
All rights reserved.
November 2019

Information + Contacts
3PRACTICES.COM

CONTENTS

1	All Men are Like That	1
2	"Stereotypes Are a Real Time-Saver"	6
3	Don't Tell Me Why, Show Me How	16
4	Please Welcome to our stage … The Three Practices	22
5	Practice One I'll be Unusually Interested in the Other	26
6	Practice Two I'll Stay in the Room with Difference	31
7	Practice Three I'll Stop Comparing My Best with Your Worst	35
8	Three Things the 3Practices Don't Do	41
9	Try This at Home	52
10	The Uncle Bob Moment	63
11	The Salt Shaker	69
12	Setting the Table	75
13	Playing the Game	83
14	Practicing the Practices	92
15	Running In Circles … But In A Good Way	96
	About the Authors	102
	Acknowledgements	103

Let's get this started…

Chapter 1 | All Men Are Like That

A woman — 60ish, light-skinned, a career schoolteacher, long-married with children — sits in a circle of 20 or so culturally similar people. She's meeting most of them for the first time. The subject of their conversation is Donald Trump and his still-new presidency.

The story takes place in Seattle, so it won't surprise you that most people in the circle are less than pleased to have Mr. Trump in the White House. Others, this woman included, express hope that Mr. Trump will, in fact, make America great again.

Someone says something like, "I'd be curious to know, given Donald Trump's bullying, misogyny, and sexual exploitations, how you explain his treatment of women to your sons?" Just that — an open-ended invitation to say more.

Her response is stunning. "All men are like that," she says.

Her husband of 30-something years, seated next to her, doesn't bat an eye.

The silence stretches awkwardly until the person guiding the conversation asks if there's someone else who would like to take a couple of minutes to say what they think about Donald Trump. The range of opinions continues about as you'd expect ... with the additional overhang of the woman's final declaration: "All men are like that."

Another half-hour passes and the conversation shifts from what people think about Donald Trump to what they think about each other — specifically, they've been invited to thank someone in the circle who exercised restraint, dignity, clarity, made them think, or asked a really good question. And it is now that the 60-something woman speaks up again, and the story turns in something more than what's on the surface.

What the woman says is: "I'd like to thank all of you for listening to me tonight ... I don't remember ever being listened-to like this. It means a lot to me."

And, with that, this story turns out to be about a woman who has come to accept bad behavior by men as a given, sitting in a circle talking with people who have agreed they won't behave badly — at least in the circle, at least toward each other. She holds opinions she anticipates will be met with frowns from at least half the people in the circle, but in less than 30 minutes she feels safe enough to take a chance, and speak her mind. And not only do her circle-mates listen respectfully, they ask for more — not because they agree or expect her to say something they've never thought of, but because she's their neighbor who they want to respect, understand and connect with.

And so she thanks them for listening in a way she can't recall experiencing in six decades.

For the last few years, we've been creating the conditions for this sort of thing to happen all over the place with all sorts of people — we could just as easily have begun this story with a 19-year-old college freshman who expressed gratitude to the circle he was in at the University of California Merced by saying, "Thank you for listening to me so respectfully ... people my age are not used to that."...

...Or the longtime resident of an upscale community who thanked another longtime resident for transparently revealing how she was reduced to sleeping in her car for months following a series of unfortunate events...

...Or the conservative 13-year-old homeschooler who decided to take her chances in a group of adults, most of them strangers to her, and ended up quoting from the letters of Thomas Jefferson and exchanging real and consequential ideas with a dyed in the wool, 65-year-old Seattle liberal....

We create those conditions in something called 3Practice Circles, where the rules that everyone agrees to ensure that no one can dominate or otherwise bully anyone ... and that everyone who wishes to speak their mind may do so with confidence that their circle-mates will ask clarifying questions that are not meant to shame or silence but rather to evoke clarity and understanding. Agreement, while it would be nice, is not a 3Practice Circle goal.

3Practice Circles are built on the 3Practices.

1. I'll be unusually interested in others
2. I'll stay in the room with difference
3. I'll stop comparing my best with your worst

If the 3Practices were musical notes, the 3Practice Circle would be the band that takes those notes and arranges them into a song everyone can sing, like We Will, We Will, Rock You!

Much as musical notes can be put to use by Beethoven or The Beatles, 3Practice Circles never end up sounding alike. One Circle uses the 3Practices to write classical and another leans toward rock. The only requirement is you have to get in the Circle to experience the song.

We've written this book to tell the story about what we're doing, and how, and why. It's a book for people who are sad, angry, and apprehensive about relationships they've lost in the culture wars. It's a book for people who are unwilling to concede that losing loved ones that way has to be our new normal.

This book explains how we learned to create safe spaces for people to understand each other without being obliged to agree, and how anyone with a particular hunger for renewing the connections they've lost can be proactive about setting the table for others who want that too.

It can be done. We're doing it. So can you....

Chapter 2 | "Stereotypes Are a Real Time-Saver"

Where you from?

Traveling in the Midwest 20 years ago, I never felt self-conscious about saying I was from Seattle.[1] In fact, I felt kind of proud to be from the city that produced Jimi Hendrix, Boeing, Bill Gates, Starbucks, REI, Nirvana, Pearl Jam and Amazon. And when friends visited Seattle

---

[1] This is not likely to trip you up, but just so you know, in this book, "I, me, and my" generally means Jim Henderson and "We, and our" generally means Jim Henderson and Jim Hancock. The exceptions are instances when "we" means "everyone," as in, "we love a good story, don't we?" because who doesn't ... or when "I" is used to express a notion like, "I won't tell if you don't" — where we don't literally mean "Jim Henderson won't tell if you don't." Neither of us could have written this book ... it took both of us. That said, Jim Henderson produced initial drafts for most of the chapters — *No small feat* (says Jim Hancock) — with first-person stories that describe his experiences. This "I/We" convention isn't the only way to organize the narrative parts of this story, it's just the way we've chosen.

from say, Atlanta, Birmingham or Kansas City I don't remember having an attitude about anything other than maybe their football team.

Times have changed. Today all we need to do is namecheck our hometown and the conversation is essentially over. In the sage words of *The Onion*, "stereotypes are a real time-saver."[2]

The difference divide that separates us has expanded to the point that we now slot those with whom we disagree into one of three categories. They're *ignorant* (needing better info), *idiots* (they know, but still refuse to acknowledge the rightness of my views) or, the most dangerous perhaps – *evil* – they're out to destroy my way of life, on a mission to hurt those I love, and committed to dismantling everything we've built to make this nation great. I must resist, and if necessary, remove them.[3]

I was sitting in a restaurant recently and overheard a mother describe California to her adult daughter as "a socialist state." Really? I need to get word to my Republican friends in Orange County and warn them. For this woman, the people of California aren't just idiots, now they're straight-up evil because that's what socialism means to her. Californians need to be written

---

[2] Wallace Rickard, "Stereotypes Are a Real Time-Saver," The Onion (https://www.theonion.com/stereotypes-are-a-real-time-saver-1819583925, 08.14.02).

[3] Kathryn Schulz and Eli Parser, TEDx Talk, "Kathryn Schulz & Eli Parser on Transparency in Thinking," (https://brainzooming.com/2011tedxkc-2011-kathryn-schulz-and-eli-parser-on-transparency-in-thinking/9103/).

off, because that's what one does when one is surrounded by evil!

America has had its breakups before — the 60s, Civil Rights, Viet Nam, Watergate, Iraq.

But something has fundamentally shifted. Something has died. We can't remember the feeling of being close — of trusting each other. We've become like rabid sports fans, proudly displaying our banners and waving our flags in each other's faces: Red State, Blue State, Pro-Choice, Pro-Life, Gay, Straight, Black Lives Matter, All Lives Matter, #metoo, #hetoo. Then we take it personally when our ideological opponents, feigning forgetfulness, mock our preferred acronyms — "I can't keep it straight: Is it LGBT or LGTB? And what's up with the Q? … or when they reject our chosen branding — "You guys aren't pro-life, you're just antiabortion!"

Sure, in polite company, we know how to appear interested. What we don't know how to do is hear each other. We've lost our innate sense of curiosity. We've stopped trusting each other. The legal separation is over. We're heading for divorce.

> Have you broken up with friends or family over political differences?
>
> Is your business suffering because key employees won't talk with each other?
>
> Have you discovered that people don't change their minds because of better information?

Has anybody thanked you for proving their idea is stupid and, by extension, so are they?

Do you want to be a nicer person?

Are you worn out from all the bickering?

It was our own experience asking these questions that drove us to seek out role models — people who demonstrated a commitment to crossing the difference divide in their organizational, familial and civic relationships. We were looking for exemplars — people who practiced the 3Practices even if they didn't call it that.

Then, in the spring of 2016, we found proof of concept from an unlikely source. Out of the blue, I got a call from a white evangelical pastor in Peoria, Illinois — America's Heartland.

Starting with touring shows in the 1890s, the phrase, "Will it play in Peoria?" became a byword for "tough audience." Meaning, if your show's a hit in Peoria, you've got a decent shot at the rest of the country. And if it bombs in Peoria? Go back to the drawing board. Jim Powell, the evangelical preacher on the phone, said he was five years into an unlikely — surprisingly close —friendship with a Peoria rabbi named Daniel Bogard, and Pastor Powell's neighbor across the church parking lot, Imam Kamil Mufti.

Reverend Powell said he and his friends wanted to talk with me about helping them write a book like the one I wrote with my atheist friend, Matt Casper.[4] Over

---

4 Jim Henderson and Matt Casper, Jim and Casper Go to Church, (Tyndale House Publishers, 2007).

several phone calls, I pressed Jim for relational details. I kept the conversations short, stretching our contacts out over a couple of weeks to give us multiple chances to opt-out. Then I asked for a conference call that would require coordinating schedules with my production partners on the West Coast and the three in Peoria.

Through it all, the Peoria Three couldn't have been more accommodating. Our conference call lasted 50 minutes, with the folks on my end posing tough questions to root out any exaggerations or soft spots in the story.

After the call, I got back on the line with my West Coast friends. We agreed that, unless the Peoria Three were practiced conspirators, their story was most likely a true expression of genuine friendship between three smart, accomplished, worldly-wise people whose racial/ethnic, national, social, political, and religious differences should have — by 2016 rules of engagement — kept them apart. It looked like these guys really were crossing the difference divide and had been doing so for half a decade.

That's why Jim Hancock and I traveled with our co-producers, Brian Boyle and Cara Highsmith, to the Midwest. If the Peoria Three were for real, we wanted to meet them face to face. More than that, if they truly were modeling behaviors that others could emulate to cross their own difference divides, we wanted to help them tell their story.

Peoria is what a lot of Americans think about when they think about the Midwest … with one wrinkle. About three-quarters of Peoria County residents are White[5] ... that number drops just below 70 percent in the city of Peoria. According to Sperling's Best Places, about 55 percent of Peorians say they are religious — a little over 43 percent identifying as Christian.[6] The wrinkle is in the next number: Across the total US population, about one percent identify as American Muslims. In Peoria, nearly 11 percent identify with Islam.[7] That concentration is about double the rate in Peoria County, and nearly four times greater than Illinois State. Business and medicine bring people from all over the world to make their homes in Peoria. In particular, the heavy equipment giant, Caterpillar, managed to attract a bunch of engineers from outside the US — many of them Muslim, or assumed to be Muslim by some of their White, native-born Illinoian neighbors — that's not characteristic of what most American's think when they think about the Midwest.

We spent a week shooting interviews with Imam Mufti, Rabbi Bogard, Reverend Powell, members of their congregations, the presidents of the mosque and the synagogue, staff at the church, leaders in business, education, religion, and city and state government.

As we dove into the footage, everything we saw and heard fed our resolve to unpack this uncommon

---

[5] US Census, QuickFacts, Peoria County, Illinois, (https://www.census.gov/quickfacts/fact/table/peoriacountyillinois/PST045218, accessed 11.04.19).

[6] Sperling's Best Places, Peoria, Illinois (https://www.bestplaces.net/religion/city/illinois/peoria, accessed 11.04.19).

[7] ibid

friendship and the outsized impact it was having on Peoria. A few weeks later, we returned for additional interviews with spouses and children of the Peoria Three, community leaders and congregants, and with a decorated US combat officer — a Purple Heart recipient — whose family were still members of the mosque led by Imam Mufti.

About 90 days later, we had the first drafts of a feature-length documentary film and book called *No Joke* (because what else would you call a story about a rabbi, an imam, and an evangelical preacher?). And 90 days after that, we had the finished products.

We took the movie out for a series of public and private institutional screenings followed by questions and answer sessions with the three friends. That led to cutting a 28-minute movie, *The Project of Us*, that enabled us to introduce audiences to the Peoria Three and the 3Practices in shorter time frames.

Whatever version of the movie we showed, regardless of the audience, and whether or not we managed to get all three of the men to the screening and Q&A, the response was overwhelmingly positive. We tried a screening of the short film when none of the Peoria Three were able to attend, followed by us, answering questions as the film producers… and that worked too.

Life is funny. You walk through a door anticipating X and before you know it, Y puts out her hand and says, "Come on in!"

We had decided — as producers, with the involvement and blessing of the Peoria Three — to frame their story around The 3Practices. We didn't want to just inspire audiences — we wanted to give people practices they could put to use immediately in their own lives. Which is why the last third of the *No Joke* movie, and all of the 28-minute short, *The Project of Us*, centers on how the three religious leaders and their communities learned to, as we like to say, practice the Practices. The Peoria Three agreed that the 3Practice terminology described what they were doing and allowed us to wrap their example in that language.

Over about 15 months, we tested what audiences wanted more of — *the band* (the Peoria Three) or *the song* (The 3Practices). As it turned out, the answer was *neither*. The audience wasn't asking for more inspiration — and the Peoria Three are nothing if not inspirational — nor were they asking for more information (the 3Practices seem easy enough to remember, and self-evident enough, once you start thinking about them, that most people don't feel the need for a deep dive ... at least not right away).

The audience asked for a third choice. What people really wanted was instruction — more show me and less tell me. Returning to our musical theme, people were saying they wanted to learn to sing the song themselves.

That's what prompted us to form a new band — we called it the 3Practice Circle. We designed 3Practice Circles from scratch to provide people a place to hear the song, sing along, and ultimately learn to play it themselves.

Since then, we've introduced the 3Practices to civic organizations, business associations, religious and inter-religious groups, schools and universities. We lead 3Practice Circles in their communities and then train 3Practice Circle Leaders to continue the work.

Like me, rock historian/critic Bob Lefsetz views life through the lens of music. I recently found this in his popular Lefsetz Letter:

> *As much as we're divided, we're looking to be brought together* [emphasis mine].
>
> We all don't have to agree, but we all want to be able to weigh in.
>
> It's those who create product that brings in everybody who will win the future.[8]

Beautiful. But don't just take a rock critic's word. The scholars agree. The *Hidden Tribes* report "provides substantial evidence of deep polarization and growing tribalism… it also provides some evidence for optimism, showing that *77 percent of Americans believe our differences are not so great that we cannot come together."* [emphasis mine].[9]

---

[8] Bob Lefsetz, "Part of the Conversation," The Lefsetz Letter, (https://lefsetz.com/wordpress/2019/05/09/part-of-the-conversation/, 05.09.19).

[9] Stephen Hawkins, Daniel Yudkin, Míriam Juan-Torres, Tim Dixon, Hidden Tribes: A Study of America's Polarized Landscape, (More In Common, Version 1.0.3, 2018), 5.

Our 3Practice Circle experiences corroborate what Lefsetz intuits and the *Hidden Tribes* report measures, which is this: There's reason for hope.

Here's why — it's what we've seen with our own eyes as we've led dozens of 3Practice Circles with all sorts of people, in all kinds of settings: When people feel the music, when they find themselves humming along, when they don't want the song to end, that's when the possibility of profound connection increases dramatically. That's when people start wondering why they used to think that disagreeing about hot button issues meant they had no choice but to break up.[10]

---

10 If this last bit leaves you feeling apprehensive ... if it makes you worry we're saying that principled disagreements don't matter ... keep reading. And if you feel really jumpy, jump ahead to the chapter eight, "Three Things the 3Practices Don't Do." By the time you finish that, we think you'll see why we think protecting good-faith convictions and maintaining healthy boundaries is super important. Chapter three, "Don't Tell Me Why — Show Me How," will be waiting for you when you get back.

Chapter 3 | Don't Tell Me Why — Show Me How

William Smith is credited with being the father of modern geology. Smith lived in England in the late 1700s where his day job was draining swamplands and digging canals. Periodically he would descend into coal mines on one of those creaky elevators. While everyone else was probably praying the ropes didn't break, Smith was busy staring at dirt.

And by and by, Smith noticed something. As the elevator slowly descended he noticed that the earth changed colors. Where others saw dirt Smith saw a whole new world hiding right out in the open, something that we now call strata.

His curiosity about strata would eventually lead him to create the first map of the entire island of England including the 27 strata it sat on.[11] William Smith's map opened up whole new industries and sources of wealth for people who began to excavate wherever he said there was coal or other valuable minerals.

Picture our current cultural landscape as 27 layers of difference, some of which lie just below the surface and others that run deep under the earth. It turns out that these layers of difference shape everything we see above ground.

What if we had a mechanism that enabled us to go beneath the surface and observe these differences up close. What if we had a map of these layers of difference and something akin to a relational elevator that took us below the surface but still managed to return us safely once our exploration was completed.

That describes what we think is happening with 3Practice Circles. They become our mechanism to travel to new places in our thinking and to see things from another viewpoint – one that is hidden from view to those who only deal with surface things.

Here's what that exploration looks like, in a 3Practice Circle.

The Framing Question that evening was: Racism: As American as Apple Pie?

About 20 people gathered in a 3Practice Circle to offer their opinions on this heated issue. A white gentleman was talking when his two minutes ran out. I said *Thank*

---

11 Learn more about William Smith in Simon Winchesters, The Map That Changed The World: William Smith and the Birth of Modern Geology, (Harper Perennial, 2009).

you, which is 3Practice code for *Please stop*, but then he asked me for a little more time to finish.

Normally at this point, I would say no and move on, but for some reason that night I nodded to him to go on. That's a Referee's prerogative but upon further review, it proved to be a bad call.

When he finished and people began asking clarifying questions, our only black friend in the group that night (remember the topic?) asked our white friend this question: "I'd be curious to know why you thought it was ok to go over your allotted time?"

Remember, as the Head Referee, I'm ultimately the one who makes the decision to give someone extra time or not, so in reality, my black friend was questioning me. Our white friend tried to explain himself, as did I, but ultimately we knew our explanations sounded weak. We were both wrong and we owned it then and there.

Another person piped up with a question for our black friend: "I'd be curious to know" she said, "why you asked that question," to which he responded, "Because I've learned to expect that white men don't think the rules apply to them. As a black man, I would not be allowed to go over my time."

The Circle sat in stunned silence for a long moment. We got the message. Systemic racism is a thing. It's real and we had just participated in it.

We end each Circle with thank-yous. During that time the white gentleman spoke to our black friend and said; "Thank you. I've literally never thought about that before. I appreciate you calling me out… I think maybe I do that all the time."

Think about that. When was the last time you sat in a group of ideological opponents who owned their bias? When was the last time you heard a man apologize and say he was wrong in public?

In our explorations, we've discovered something about people who get along — and even cooperate — with their ideological opponents. Like William Smith, we found it hidden in plain sight. So, we're not saying it's easy … but we won't be surprised if you think it's obvious once we share it.

What we discovered can be expressed as *three Practices and one Skill* that help people tell the truth and hear the truth in adversarial relationships. Here again, are the practices — we'll go into more detail later:

> The First Practice is… I'll be unusually interested in others
>
> The Second Practice is… I'll stay in the room with difference
>
> The Third Practice is… I'll stop comparing my best with your worst

The Skill we teach is disciplined curiosity, wrapped up in the five-word phrase, "I'd be curious to know." Think of this phrase as a relational safety pin — that incredibly modest device we keep out of sight but close at hand for just-in-time assistance when we're about to "lose it," or when things "start slipping" … like that time when a close friend mentions they voted for the candidate you think is the worst person in the world or mocks an issue you just donated money to support. You know, those moments when you get "triggered." "I'd be curious to know," is really handy in circumstances you can't control — especially with a relative, friend, boss or fellow employee with whom you have a significant connection.

That's what happened between my wife and a young relative during the George W. Bush presidency. My wife was adamantly against the Iraq war. Her disgust drove her to go door to door to help elect Barack Obama. During a large family gathering, one of our young relatives expressed her dislike for Obama and my wife went off on her. You can picture the scene I'm sure. My wife felt terrible and immediately apologized to the younger woman. They patched things up but my wife went away determined to not let that happen again. But how would she turn good intentions into reliable civility?

What we've come to understand is that we don't need lofty ideals. What we need are practices and skills — doable behaviors we can consciously practice in the context of our ordinary lives … skills that can serve, like that relational safety pin, when contentious issues threaten to cause our relationship with a loved one to come apart at the seams.

Don't Tell Me Why — Show Me How! That's what we kept hearing from the people who watched our *No Joke* film or read the book. Of course people were inspired by the Peoria Three's courage and love for each other. But when everyone has YouTube in their pocket, inspiration is cheap and easy to access. What's not so easy, and what people keep telling us they want, is instructions on how to play in the band not just watch it.

Maybe, like me, you're old enough remember where you were when The Beatles appeared on the Ed Sullivan Show. Sure, there were millions of people who were satisfied with screaming, but there were also thousands of people who decided right then and there to pick up a guitar and join a band. And every one of them needed a guitar teacher or a patient friend to help them learn to play what they were hearing in their heads ... and help them keep going when they hit the wall and wanted to quit.

That's why we kept hacking the 3Practices and tinkering over and over with the design of the 3Practice Circle. We wanted to make sure that whatever we added or eliminated would help people integrate the 3Practices into their everyday routine. We wanted them to be able to pick up a guitar, learn a few chords, join a band and start singing their own tunes.

Chapter 4 | Please Welcome to Our Stage … The 3Practices

"Attention is the rarest and purest form of generosity." — Simone Weil

Human beings learn by doing.

That's why we talk about three practices, not three principles, philosophies, beliefs or theories.

We purposely use (some might say overuse) the word "practices" to drive that point home.

I've never forgotten seeing these words on a poster decades ago…

You can act your way to a new set of feelings faster than you can feel your way to a new set of actions.

I'm impressed by the speed and strength of people playing NFL-level football. I'm astounded by the physical prowess of NBA-level players. I'm amazed by world-class soccer players who score goals with their feet and their heads. I'm captivated by great orators, and in awe of base-jumping skydivers. However, I am under no illusion that I'll be following in their footsteps, ever.

Ordinary, everyday working people lack the time, energy, motivation, and talent to perform feats of strength, eloquence, and high-flying acrobatics. We pay to watch others do those things. They entertain us, then we yawn and go to bed. Some of us yawn and go to bed because we've set an alarm to wake us up in time to go the gym first thing in the morning.

Ordinary people don't need to master professional athletic skills and practices in their pursuit of ordinary fitness. They need simple, doable skills and practices suitable to their age, health, and physical capabilities.

You can see where this is going: Ordinary people don't need big ideas about peace, love, and understanding, they need simple, doable skills they can put into practice immediately to cross the difference divide with people in their relational networks. With that as our standard, Jim Hancock and I set out to "stare" … not at dirt, like William Smith, the father of geology, but at people. Specifically, we stared at people who, by practice, had become very good at crossing the difference divide in their personal and professional relationships. Our task? Observe them and write down, not what they say so much as what they do, and then turn that information into a map that people who want to follow in their footsteps can use.[12] When you open a map, it's a bonus if it's pretty. What you really want is clear and specific directions about how to get from where you are to where you want to be, and back again.

In the process of developing all this, we discovered that even if a practice is primarily internal (like meditation), if it's going to "stick," it needs to be connected to an external behavior (like mindful breathing). New behaviors can be challenging but they must also be doable. Learning to breathe in a way that assists meditation takes practice, but it's doable. Learning to listen with disciplined curiosity is likewise doable ... it just takes practice.

We observed many examples of crossing the difference divide but ultimately condensed it down to three practices, exhibited by people who cross the difference divide

---

[12] At this point, we want to own what's obvious. We know you know we're a couple of old, straight, white guys, with all the cultural privileges attached to that situation. If you intuit a air of patriarchy in what we say and how we say it, please know that we're trying to understand and take on the responsibilities that properly attach to our unearned privilege — including the responsibility to learn from, collaborate with, and be mutually accountable to people who are not old, straight white guys. We believe we may be making modest progress in this journey. And, having shifted the metaphor in this chapter from William Smith's vertical geological map to a horizontal geographical map, we feel compelled to add that, if you sniff an undertone of colonization, we absolutely do not intend it. The 3Practices are not meant to lend the slightest support to any doctrine of conquest. If anything, we're persuaded that heartfelt curiosity, tolerance for differences, and treating ideological opponents as human equals repudiates the colonial impulse to otherize, plunder, exploit, and then assimilate, scatter, and destroy people. If there is a map across the difference divide it charts borders that are open to traffic in all directions.

repeatedly and on purpose — whether in a family, at work, school, community, or a house of worship. The context may change but the practices remain the same.

Let's review The Three Practices.

> Practice One. I'll be unusually interested in others
>
> Practice Two. I'll stay in the room with difference
>
> Practice Three. I'll stop comparing my best with your worst

In the following pages, we'll illustrate each Practice with a story and offer several exercises you can use to practice the Practice while you reconnect with a friend, family member, or colleague you don't want to lose.

Chapter 5 | Practice One

I'll be unusually interested in others

Princess Shaw was all but invisible. But, being a resourceful if poor millennial singer-songwriter Princess turned to YouTube and posted videos of herself performing. Thanks to the magic of social media (and unbeknownst to her), all the way over in Israel, an artist/producer named Kutiman, took a very unusual level of interest in her work. He began to write arrangements and record her tunes. Ultimately their unusual relationship became the subject of the documentary film, *Presenting Princess Shaw*. By the end of the film, we see Princess in Israel, meeting Kutiman and performing live with him.

That Kutiman-kind of attention doesn't happen for everyone… but most of us have received some special attention at least once in our lives.

Did you have a teacher or a coach who noticed you, paid attention or *saw* you? How old were you at the time? Do you still remember their name or see their face in your mind's eye? Why, after all these years, is that memory still fresh? Could it be because, as Simone Weil said, attention is the rarest and purest form of generosity?

It's rare because… well, it just doesn't happen that often — it's not an everyday experience. It's pure because the impact is private and deeply personal. Oftentimes the person "paying" attention isn't even aware they're doing it. They're just being like Kutiman … someone who sees something in you and decides to tell you what they see.

I recently attended a memorial service for a woman who had been delightfully candid with me when I was just starting out in my career. At her service, I mentioned regretting not listening more closely to her advice since, as it turned out, she was wiser than I'd appreciated at the time. A few weeks later, I received a message from her daughter who told me, "Hey, I thought you'd like to know, a few months before my mom passed she mentioned that there were two men in her life who really listened to her, and you were one of them — so don't be so hard on yourself!" It turns out that even though I felt like I hadn't done enough, it was apparently more than she got from others so it stood out. You never know when someone's watching you listen to them.

David Augsburger captures the essence of this experience with his powerful insight, "Being heard is so close to being loved that for the average person they are almost indistinguishable."[13] Isn't that your experience? When you talk about being loved isn't it amazingly similar to that feeling you get when someone listens closely to you or pays attention to you? The two experiences – being listened to and being loved— are so intermingled that most us of can't tell them apart.

How do we develop the practice of being unusually interested in others? How can we use it to cross the difference divide?

Boiled down, being unusually interested in others simply means we out-listen people. And how do we learn how to do that? The same way we learned how to play in a band or speak a foreign language — we practice.

Here are techniques, exercises, methods and hacks you can use to practice being unusually interested in others.

Count to Three
In the context of your normal encounters with people, after asking a question, give them a few seconds to respond before answering it yourself. Here's how. Silently count to three (one-one thousand, two-one thousand, three-one thousand) before telling them your thoughts. Here's another way: Silently repeat "bah, bah black sheep have you any wool" in your mind. That will take about three seconds and you'll be done!

---

13 David W. Augsburger, Caring Enough to Hear and Be Heard, (Regal Books, 1982), 12.

Out-listen people – don't let them let you have the last word.

Sit with silence – do the internal work – feel the awkwardness.

If you're anything like me, you'll LOL when you realize how challenging this exercise is.

Ask the Second Question
If you've watched a presidential press conference you've seen reporters ask a question and, just as the president is about to finish his answer, they cut in with, "I have a follow-up question; did you . . ." Follow-up questions are powerful because you invite a person to "tell me more." When you circle back and ask the second question, it signals that you're genuinely curious. It tells them that you're actually listening closely. Asking the second question is an act of generosity and kindness — a gift — and for those in organizations, the information gleaned from follow-up questions often proves to have enormous value. In some instances, you may be able to plan the second question before you ask the first one — but don't let that get in the way of listening.

Nudge them with "Please tell me more..." or "I'd like to hear more about that..."
Human beings are attention junkies. Given the encouragement, they rarely turn down the opportunity to elaborate or explain why they think the world would be a better place if we drove the kind of car they own, watched the movies they've seen, ate the food they love and voted for the candidate they support.

Nudge 'em with a little, "Please tell me more."

They'll seldom disappoint.

Chapter 6 | Practice Two

I'll stay in the room with difference

If we had to capture the essence of the 3Practices in one Practice it would be *Staying in the room with difference.*

The practice of staying in the room with difference is most easily understood this way. You discover that I voted for the wrong person and we don't break up.

Mike and Lily are a dad and daughter living in Iowa. He's a single dad and she's a young student. He's a staunch conservative, and she wants to be a politician — but her dad says he won't vote for her. "I didn't know what to do with that information. I just kind of sat there," Lily recalls. "I don't think I talked to him for a while after that." Mike didn't understand what he said wrong.

"After that I kind of realized it was a losing fight," Lily says. Changing her dad's mind "wasn't something I should continue to pursue, because if he wouldn't even vote for his own daughter, there's no way I was gonna be able to convince him otherwise on anything."[14]

It may not look pretty but this dad/daughter duo is trying to stay in the room with difference. They could use a few tips on how to make understanding more likely and less ugly but at least they're trying. This is the first step — you decide to not leave. You decide to find a way to stay connected without abandoning your convictions. You give up on common ground and start searching for uncommon ground.

A few years ago, on an earlier exploration of crossing the difference divide, I enlisted a gentleman named Matt Casper to help me review and critique some of the biggest churches in America.[15] Matt's a marketer by trade and an atheist by choice. We became good friends and wrote two books together. It was a delightful, exhilarating, and transformative experience for both of us. As we traveled around the country sharing our story, we decided that instead of arguing about a God he didn't believe in and I wasn't smart enough to convince him existed, we would practice staying in the room with difference, and talk about that choice in public. That's finding uncommon ground.

---

[14] Jessica Testa, "She's 17 And Wants To Be A Politician. Her Dad Says He Won't Vote For Her," (Buzzfeed News, https://www.buzzfeednews.com/article/jtes/shes-17-and-wants-to-be-a-politician-her-dad-says-he-wont, 01.16.18).

[15] Jim Henderson and Matt Casper, Jim and Casper Go to Church, (Tyndale House Publishers, 2007).

In a 3Practice Circle titled Gun Rights or Gun Laws? Robert asked Ella this clarifying question after she shared her opinion: "I'd be curious to know if you think your passionate advocacy for, as you put it, 'sane gun laws' is in any way similar to the Pro-life Movement's passion for what they call the 'rights of the unborn'?" Ella paused and said, "That's a great question. I hadn't seen them as equivalent, but hmmm… you're making me think." After the group, Ella and Robert privately continued to process the issue. As I watched from a distance, I reflected on just exactly how far apart these two people were in their viewpoints. Robert was probably "packing heat" and would be quite comfortable representing the NRA. Ella on the other hand, was a bra-burning liberal from the 60s. Yet, here they were, actually talking and practicing staying in the room with difference. Neither of them seemed likely to change their mind about the "facts," but they appeared to be quickly changing their minds about each other. Staying in the room with difference pays dividends you don't see coming at first because when people like each other the rules change.

Here are techniques, exercises, methods and hacks you can use to practice staying in the room with difference.

Bookend Your Opinion
Begin your next on- or offline rant with IMHO (In My Humble Opinion), and end it with BICBW (But I Could Be Wrong). That's how you'll know you're practicing staying in the room with difference. You might feel like you're pretending but, like they say in AA, "fake it 'til you make it."

Co-Belligerate Whenever Possible

Belligerence is antagonism against something or someone. Co-belligerence involves ideological opponents mutually directing antagonism toward a shared obstacle or enemy — working together to accomplish a shared goal. When ideological opponents join forces against a mutual enemy, powerful things can happen.

A number of years ago a friend introduced me to Rob Smith. Rob and I harbor significant political and philosophical differences and typically fall on opposite ends of the ideological spectrum, but we united around a common goal. Rob and I agreed that the harmful influence of a religious leader in our city needed to be stopped.

Rob Smith and I became comrades, allies, and co-belligerents in the fight to publicly remove a religious bully — Rob from the inside, me from the outside. We formed a very public, respectful relationship around this shared goal.[16] After six weeks of shining a bright light on the abusive nature of the bully's operations, he resigned.

Over time, Rob and I became personal friends. He was instrumental in helping us start the first 3Practice Circle. Co-belligerating around a shared purpose led to a life-changing friendship.

---

[16] You can learn more about this story in Jim Henderson and Doug Murren's, Question Mark, (90-Day Books, 2015).

Chapter 7 | Practice 3

I'll stop comparing my best with your worst

If only he hadn't written: "all men are created equal," we might be able to give Thomas Jefferson a pass. Unfortunately, the historical record does not lie in this matter. Here's the truth: Thomas Jefferson bought and sold slaves, all the while condemning others for buying and selling slaves.

Amazingly, Jefferson managed to gloss over his own insidious behavior, even as he lambasted his most famous ideological opponent, King George of England:

> This piratical warfare, the opprobrium of infidel powers, is the warfare of the CHRISTIAN king of Britain. Determined to keep open a market where MEN should be bought and sold, he has

prostituted his negative for suppressing every legislative attempt to prohibit or to restrain this execrable commerce. [emphasis Jefferson's][17]

This is Jefferson comparing his best with King George's worst... Ever done that? I have.

As Kathryn Schultz points out in her powerful book, *Being Wrong*, "We positively excel at acknowledging other people's errors."[18]

Later in our history, during the run-up to the Civil War, though many northerners were certainly vocal about the evils of slavery, their protest often stopped there. Why? Because, while the economy of the northern states could not be directly linked to slave labor, it can be readily argued that northern consumers and businesses in most categories benefitted profoundly thanks to cheap imports from slave states.[19] This lip-service-only advocacy of ending slavery did not escape the notice of southerners, meaning whenever northerners criticized southern slaveholders, it fell on deaf ears. A lot like it does today.

---

[17] Thomas Jefferson, "Rough Draft of the Declaration of Independence," The Papers of Thomas Jefferson, Volume 1: 1760-1776, (Princeton University Press, 1950), 423-28.

[18] Kathryn Schultz, Being Wrong (HarperCollins, 2010), 8

[19] Michael Emerson and Christian Smith write: "On the whole northern evangelicals did not differ from southern evangelicals in their racial views, except that they tended to oppose slavery. This was easily done, in that slavery did not exist in the North." Michael O. Emerson and Christian Smith, Divided By Faith: Evangelical Religion and the Problem of Race in America (Oxford University Press, 2000), 34.

What if, instead of acting as if they were better than southerners, the northerners had owned their duplicity and invited their southern fellow citizens to grant slaves freedom and then join forces with them to offer former slaves employment at fair wages. How might that have changed our history? We'll never know.

It's become apparent that a pattern of re-litigating the American Civil War continues right up to our time. Where would politics, not to mention cable news, be without this rich vein of division to draw upon?

A 3Practice Circle held in a conservative community touched on this divide.

Tom is one of those people who takes notes in meetings — which, when you're the one talking, can make you feel either intimidated or like the most important person in the room. Tom got us started. "The president is not your run-of-the-mill politician. He's definitely draining the swamp back there in DC." If Tom harbored a shred of doubt, it didn't show, plus, his effusive optimism made you like him, whether you agreed with him or not. The group asked Tom a couple of clarifying questions, which he answered politely and confidently, then the conversation moved on to Frank who couldn't have disagreed more with Tom.

Frank decided the group needed some balance, so he let loose with a litany of reasons the President was the most dangerous man in America and must be impeached. Following Frank's time, Tom quietly asked if there was any middle ground in his thinking, and Frank assured him no, none at all. In a 3Practice Circle, there are no follow-up responses or retorts, so Tom remained quiet.

As we closed the Circle we asked people to share their personal takeaways. Tom raised his hand and said, "As I listened, I realized that sometimes I think things are facts that might not actually be facts. I need to think about that more."

The group sat quietly. The Circle leader thanked Tom for being transparent and self-effacing. She pointed out that Tom had just modeled Practice Three — I'll stop comparing my best with your worst. Why? Because Tom didn't have to share anything. He was on the winning team—his guy was in the Oval Office. But something about the Circle invited him to be more open about his working assumptions.

Tom invited his ideological opponent to help him see something. He made himself vulnerable. Most of the time we do the opposite. We try and one-up our ideological opponents by finding a weakness in their argument. Instead, Tom openly admitted to the Circle that he might have something to learn from the people his team had just defeated. Tom stopped "playing gotcha" and instead "gave ground," which can be the first step in creating dialogue.

Here are techniques, exercises, methods, and hacks, you can use to practice not comparing your best with their worst.

Give Away Your Advantage
I think Father Greg Boyle is a hero for his innovative work with gang members in LA. I once heard a CNN interviewer ask him, "Aren't you concerned they'll take advantage of you?" Father Boyle's response was perfect. "No," he said, "I gave my advantage away." He let them take advantage of him; he let them win.

Next time you find yourself in an argument about a contentious issue you feel passionate about, think about Father Boyle and practice giving your advantage away. Here's how: When your ideological opponent makes a good point against your side, instead of retaliating (which anybody can do), let them know they made you think about your own assumptions. Instead of a verbal show of force, let them have the last word. You will experience the visceral feeling of not comparing your best with their worst.

Atrocity Industry and Outrage Culture
The Cable news business rests on the pillars of outrage and atrocity. Name which network you watch. Who's your favorite culture translator (a.k.a. news personality)? Who is it that you trust? Whose reputation is unassailable in your mind? Who presents news in a way that is evidence-based, smart and honest? People are drawn to networks that reliably expose their ideological opponents' most outrageous claims and keep them updated on a minute-by-minute basis of the atrocities committed by the other side. In fact, most of us have never watched the other guy's network because they are known liars, every one of them, who purposely mislead people and are essentially just a propaganda machine for

some rich elites' agenda. The people who watch that channel are uncritical and never acknowledge views that run counter to their party line.

It would feel disloyal and maybe even "sinful" to give those people the time of day.

Here's a really fast way to see how close you are to being able to practice not comparing your best with their worst: Turn on the other channel. Watch their most popular commentator. They'll be easy to find since they're on the air at the exact same time as your most popular commentator so you can click between them. Write down statements made by the other side and compare them with your team's claims. Take particular note when they make "any" concession or acknowledge the existence of an alternative view other than their own. "Force" yourself to listen to at least one complete segment and compare and contrast the similarities or differences on the two channels. That's how it feels to begin to stop comparing your best with your ideological opposites' worst.

Chapter 8 | Three Things The 3Practices Don't Do

When we say Yes to the 3Practices, there are, simultaneously, three things to which we say No.

1. Surrender

Crossing the difference divide doesn't require you to surrender your beliefs, abandon your convictions, or change your mind.

In fact, the opposite is true. Owning your opinions, values, and beliefs — while staying connected to your ideological opposite — is the revolutionary shift 3Practice Circles are designed to facilitate.

In his book *A Failure of Nerve*, Edwin Friedman borrows a concept from biology, called *differentiation*, and applies it to leadership development. Friedman says a well-differentiated leader is someone:

> who has clarity about his or her own life goals
>
> who can be separate while still remaining connected
>
> who can manage his or her own reactivity in response to the automatic reactivity of others and, therefore be able to take stands at the risk of displeasing.[20]

Differentiating sounds admirable but it can be tricky to put into practice.

On one hand, who doesn't love feeling free to express opinions without fear of judgment?

On the other hand, for a lot of us, that's a rare experience. Many of us withhold our opinions — maybe even pretend we don't have opinions about things that, in truth, matter to us quite a lot — for the simple reason that we are afraid of losing friends. We're effectively scared silent.

Is it possible to design a communication experience that enables people to speak their minds without risking reprisal or abandonment? And if it is possible, can the experience be scaled to include different kinds of people from all sorts of backgrounds and cultures?

---

[20] Edwin H. Friedman, Margaret M. Treadwell, Edward W. Beal, A Failure of Nerve, (Church Publishing, Inc., 2007), 14.

Our answer is Yes ... maybe not 100% unconditionally guaranteed, yes-in-all-times-and-places-with-people-of-every-sort, kumbaya ... but Yes, most of the time, with most people, under most circumstances.

We know this because that's the way we designed, tested, and refined 3Practice Circles to work — starting with an unalterable commitment that no one has to surrender sincerely- held narratives, opinions, or values in order to participate wholeheartedly, so long as their values don't involve bullying, menacing, or otherwise intentionally harming others. More on this in a moment...

Along the way, we've found that substantive exchanges require strong opinions, along with receptive listeners – people who temporarily abandon their "right" to pass judgment and instead choose principled inquiry — what Cooperrider and Srivastva call "appreciative inquiry."[21]

The moments that emerge when this combination works are magical. But they're not magic. These moments of clarity are doable and repeatable. All you need to do is practice, and when people practice, they can connect in surprising and even profitable ways.

Here's what we mean by that.

Andrew Himes is a convinced progressive whose work addresses carbon-driven climate change. Rob Smith —

---

[21] Cooperrider, D. L. & Srivastva, S. (1987). "Appreciative inquiry in organizational life", In Woodman, R. W. & Pasmore, W.A. (eds.). Research in Organizational Change And Development, Vol. 1, (Stamford, CT: JAI Press), 129–169.

my co-belligerent in resisting the bullying pastor in chapter six — is a committed conservative who runs in circles with people who are skeptical of some of the climate science Andy Himes takes as evidence-based fact. Rob and Andy have both been deeply involved in the development of 3Practice Circles from the outset. They're both business people, and they both share a passion to change the world for the better. They disagree at a lot of very important points. But the points at which they agree are important enough to make them like each other.

Rob and Andy talked over lunch recently about the projects they were working on. Rob was raising money to build a community of 50 tiny houses for homeless people and Andy was raising money to launch an initiative to ensure that all new buildings constructed in the US use zero carbon in both the building process and in their operation. As the two men talked, it occurred to them that they should think about combining their resources to build fifty carbon-neutral tiny houses for homeless people. Neither of them needed to surrender their core principles in able to hear the other on that subject. Connecting on a human level opened the possibility of a new, profitable, partnership.

Think about it. What if you were able to give progressives and conservatives a way to stop arguing and start listening to each other? What new creative designs could emerge? If making the world a better place isn't your thing, then how about training your teams in the 3Practices in order to gain strategic market advantage over your competitors?

Bottom Line: participating in the 3Practice Circle requires you to bring your opinions, not surrender them.

2. Agreement

The 3Practices do not focus on getting people to surrender core beliefs, ideas, and values. They also do not focus on finding agreement.

The Peoria Three, our heroes in the *No Joke* project,[22] connected at first because of mutual interest. Each of them had expertise in something the others wanted — special insight into a sacred text. What began with intellectual curiosity, led to a path on which they discovered that, in spite of their sharply different beliefs, they actually liked each other. Each of them learned to admire the other two for their honesty, intelligence, and good will ... their disagreements were punctuated with laughter and good-natured teasing ... they found common ground in the complications of leading congregations day-to-day ... the Rabbi and the Preacher enjoyed Cardinal's baseball on TV, and the Imam joined in — though he would much rather watch cricket — because he enjoyed their company. And so they became fast friends. But, half a decade on, their friendship would be tested, not from the inside but by outside forces.

In the run-up to the 2016 presidential election, Islamophobia became a national issue. It also became an intensely local concern for the Peoria Three when Imam

---

[22] Learn more at www.nojokeproject.com

Mufti and his community began to experience open harassment on the streets of Peoria. After decades of mostly peaceful tolerance, Peoria's Muslim citizens began hearing threatening language from white neighbors. There were harrowing incidents of Muslims being run off the road by white drivers — this happened to the Imam's spouse. Strangers told Muslims to go back to where they came from. This was shocking to people like our friend, Mir Ali, who grew up in mid-80s/90s-era Peoria, never sensing disapproval, let alone being mistreated. Peoria is where Mir came from — Peoria is home.

The abuse of Muslims in Peoria escalated following a terrorist attack at a San Bernardino California County office building in December 2015. Our friend Imam Mufti has long publicly declared — in his teaching, preaching, writing, and online videos — that (as he put it in a February 2015 current affairs piece in the online magazine *Muslim Matters*) "every sane Muslim" knows that violence in the name of God or the Prophet is a violation of Islam ... a position he defended with chapter and verse from the Qur'an. Fourteen months earlier, in October 2014, Imam Mufti wrote a public letter to Christian pastors, friends and neighbors in Peoria denouncing ISIS for "recent atrocities committed in the name of our religion," saying,

> ISIS' expulsion of Christians from the Iraqi city of Mosul is a reprehensible, vile act not allowed in our religion." ... "ISIS' indiscriminate killing, destruction of houses of worship, treatment of prisoners and women, and fanatic extremism has

left us in shock and disgust. Such actions have nothing to do with Islam, whose principles call for tolerance, kindness, justice, and coexistence.

Imam Mufti was a strong voice among tens of thousands of imams and Muslim scholars who publicly condemned ISIS, but going into 2016, a different narrative was gaining traction in Peoria, fueling hate speech and threatening acts against Muslims.

This is the point when, because they were friends, and had been for half-a-decade, the Peoria Three decided to go public. In consultation with leaders in business, religion, and elected officials in city, county, and state government, they organized a city-wide gathering called Peace for Peoria which was attended by the mayor, city councilpersons, state senators, the CEO of Caterpillar, Inc, and 1000 others citizens in a show of support for Peoria's Muslim population. A few months later, at the urging of community leaders, another "Meet your Muslim Neighbor" event followed, drawing 700 people. These public events didn't put an end to the hostility some felt and expressed toward American Muslim neighbors (nor Jewish neighbors for that matter, who were also targeted by hate speech … in 2016, the Rabbi, who had earlier in the year moved from Peoria to Cincinnati, was targeted online, by name, by a nationalist hate group).

When a preacher, a rabbi and an imam in the United States become friends, people will talk — some with appreciation, some with puzzlement, some with grumbling, some with sharp criticism, some with hate. The Peoria Three experienced mixed reactions from their religious circles, ranging from the enthusiastic support of people who live and work alongside "the other," to outright rejection for openly aligning with groups holding "doctrinally deviant" beliefs. The pressure was real. Jim Powell, the evangelical pastor saw over 100 people leave his church.

Here's the interesting thing. Even though these men took a deep dive into each other's religious culture, and though the pastor and the rabbi paid a steep price, personally and professionally, for standing up for the imam and his community — even though they went that far — none of them changed their core beliefs one iota. Each of them told us the other two helped him become a better Muslim, a better Jew, a better Christian — not just where they agreed, but in their principled disagreements.

Even as we came to believe these three men would probably die for each other, it was always clear that they don't agree about something as fundamental as whether they pray to the same God. In fact, out of respect for each other, because they disagree, they don't pray together or preach in each other's congregations (they've done some teaching back and forth, but no preaching, and no attempts at interfaith worship). The rabbi remains one hundred percent Jewish in faith and practice, the imam continues in the way of the Prophet Muhammad, and the evangelical preacher still believes Jesus is *the* way, *the* truth, and *the* life. Ultimately, the only thing all three of them ended up abandoning was the bundle of stereotypes they had before they came to really know each other.

Agreement is overrated. It appears to have little or nothing to do with why human beings bond with one another. I've been married almost 50 years and my super-smart wife and I still don't agree on a lot of stuff. How about you? The truth seems to be that the people we love the most may be the ones we disagree with the most... but we still don't break up...at least half of us don't☺

That's why, while 3Practice Circles are not designed to deliver agreement, they do deliver...

Clarity

Understanding

Compassion (maybe)

Connection (frequently)

And frankly, that's all we really hope for.

When agreement happens... it's a happy surprise.

3. Abuse
The 3Practices do not focus on getting people to surrender core ideas, beliefs, and values, and they don't focus on getting people to agree with ideological opponents.

The 3Practices are not designed to tolerate abuse.

Should I practice staying in the room with a bully?

Is being unusually interested in someone who demonstrates a willingness to manipulate or otherwise inflict harm just another word for codependency?

Can I stop comparing my best with others' worst and still confront injustice where I see it?

To be sure, when conversations get heated, the line between a difference of opinion and bullying may be blurry, and good people can disagree about where that line is located.

Just as surely, there are times when it becomes impossible to engage with or remain neutral about an ideological opponent's words and/or actions.

We will go into more detail about this later. For now, suffice it to say that one important way 3Practice Circles discourage abusive language or gestures is by restricting the amount of time people are allotted to express an opinion and/or ask a clarifying question. Anyone who wants to defend or advance a point of view is obliged to engage others in the Circle. Otherwise, no one will be curious to know more and the Circle will shift their attention to the next person. In practice, once people see how the process works, they tend to relax into the flow, knowing they need to be clear, but since they will almost certainly be asked a clarifying question, inviting them to say more, they don't have to say everything they know in their two minutes.

It seems likely that someday we'll encounter someone so belligerent that we'll need to insist that he or she leave the room if they refuse to be civil. But, so far, nothing like that has happened. In fact, at one university event, administrators purposely left out a person whose obnoxious behavior, both live and online, was disruptive for everyone involved (except, presumably, his cheering section). Sure enough, when we invited volunteers from the audience to join the 3Practice fishbowl, he stepped right up … and was a perfect gentleman for the duration, staying on the subject and asking decent clarifying questions with no eye-rolling, sighing, huffing, or other displays of impatience or disapproval. Had they not told us the backstory, we would never have guessed it.

At the time of this writing, in many dozens of 3Practice Circles, this design has enabled us to take on a host of volatile topics without a single significant incident of abuse … not that people aren't sometimes offended or triggered, but 3Practice Circle Leaders will never permit personal insults to go unchallenged.

All that to say, practicing the 3Practices doesn't mean you have to stay in the room with a bully, or be unusually interested in a narcissist, or stop comparing your best with an abuser's or criminal's worst.

Chapter 9 | Try This At Home

A critical design requirement built into the 3 Practices is the capacity to travel.

There's a nagging question behind this design decision: *Why are aspirational listening techniques so rarely practiced by ordinary people?* For example, when was the last time you overheard a couple of blue-collar guys pondering the meaning of *dialogue* over a beer?

If the 3 Practices work only in the lab, under controlled conditions — if they work only in 3 Practice Circles led by experts — what good are they, really?

We need a model of dialogue that's robust enough to travel through uncontrolled environments and into unanticipated situations — relational contexts and situations where ordinary, working-class people live their real lives.

We need useful things — tools like that relational safety pin, "I'd be curious to know" — that people can pull out of their pockets and use to hold themselves together when a family member triggers them at Thanksgiving, or a workmate expresses enthusiasm for a political candidate they think is unpatriotic, idiotic, or a straight-up danger to democracy.

D.I.Y
At large events, we present the 3Practice Circle in a "fishbowl" — eight volunteers demonstrating what a 3Practice Circle looks like, while 50, or a hundred, or a thousand people watch and listen in. A 3Practice fishbowl is not the most natural setting for unfettered conversation, but somehow it works — people like being in the Circle, and folks in the audience enjoy the experience too, even though it's not immersive in the way a "real" 3Practice Circle is.

Our fishbowls manage to deliver a pretty good sense of what community-based 3Practice Circles are like. What they don't deliver is a good way for us to meet people in the audience, nor do we get the opportunity to meet-up at another 3Practice Circle a few weeks later. So there's no easy way for us to hear people's stories about practicing the Practices in real life. Still, every now and then a story catches up with us through an email or phone call. This is one of those stories, from Anita Hellam, Executive Director for Habitat for Humanity in Stanislaus County, California and a senior fellow in the Great Valley

Chapter of the American Leadership Forum (ALF)[23] who hosted a 3Practice fishbowl in Merced, California. Anita brought 20 Habitat co-workers with her to the ALF event, and sent us this story a few days later:

> One of the ladies who works in our ReSTore[24] has four little ones under 10. The day after the 3Practice workshop, she came into my office and shared that while she was cooking dinner the kids got into a loud yelling match. She stopped everything and pulled out chairs and put them in a circle. She used her timer and gave all the kids a chance to speak and ask questions. By dinner, the entire argument had been completely resolved. She told me that she feels empowered and grateful. She told me that this was a training that helps not just at work but in her personal life too.

So, let's reverse-engineer this. A mom sits in an audience of 150 people, watching a Circle of eight folks on a stage. She listens in as we offer anyone in the Circle the opportunity to take two minutes to respond to one of our favorite topics, "Racism... as American as Apple Pie?" She notices that anyone in the group may ask a

---

[23] California's Central Valley is home to a richly diverse population of Americans. ALF senior fellows — who lead organizations across a striking mix of large, medium, and small businesses, educational, medical, and religious institutions, government agencies, and nonprofits — are, in their own words, "Dedicated to joining and strengthening established leaders in order to serve the public good." We're not affiliated with ALF, we're just big on what they do (alfgreatvalley.org).

[24] ReSTore outlets upcycle used home improvement items, fixtures, and found art — if you're lucky enough to show up on the right day, it's an interior designer's dream store.

clarifying question as long as it starts with "I'd be curious to know." As with every 3Practice Circle, we conclude by inviting people to thank someone; and then we close. This is all she sees.

Nevertheless, this mom is able to take that home and immediately apply what she learned in the session! She intuitively knows how to translate what she saw in an exchange about racism to whatever it is her children are squabbling over that has everyone on edge, including her. Only now she has a new tool in her pocket that helps her hold things together with four hungry, squirrelly kids.

That's what I mean when I say the 3Practices are designed to travel.

Like CrossFit for Civility
This country was founded by people with competing ideological views. They approached the American experiment with very different outcomes in mind. Some wanted what Great Britain had. Some wanted one man, one vote governance. Some wanted to maintain slavery, while others wanted to abolish it. Their differences were not trivial, and the compromises between the founders rankled many, so much so that, less than a hundred years on, those differences exploded into America's bloodiest conflict, a civil war that technically ended in 1865 but festers to this day.

In our time, more than a few Americans wonder if we could devolve into another civil war. On the fringe, a dangerous few hope for it. Otherization has become a fact of life (I define otherization as the categorization, minimization, and defamation of people who are not like me). On the whole, we've demonstrated that we are in no condition to be good neighbors. We've forgotten how to listen, how to be curious, and how to be empathic toward our ideological opposites.

When someone is in poor physical condition, friends point them to the gym. *Go; do the work ... we can't run, or stretch, or lift weights for you, but we're behind you.* But where do you send a nation that seems dangerously unfit for the daily routines of citizenship? Where's the rehab for that?

That's why we sometimes refer to the 3Practice Circle as CrossFit for Civility.

CrossFit takes an extreme, focused and spare approach to physical exercise. Shiny StairMasters, treadmills, elliptical trainers and spandex are banned. The workout studios are typically unadorned warehouses. Big wooden boxes, large ropes, heavy pieces of steel and truck tires are strewn across concrete floors. The physical assets are spare, but the human assets are abundant. The presence of co-strugglers who are doing the work themselves — people who honestly understand and encourage newcomers, no matter what shape they're in — is a powerful source of support and encouragement.

3Practice Circles take a similarly spartan approach. No fancy constructs — just a stripped-down set of rules for keeping people safe while they push the boundaries of difference. We make participants work hard to find clarifying questions instead of conclusive arguments. We leverage everyday issues lying about in plain sight to create resistance that builds emotional muscle memory. People discover and feel the burn in underused muscles of empathy, humility, and gratitude. Fear of the other dissipates as they strengthen those muscles and learn to use them, not only in the workout but more importantly, in their routines of daily living.

For most of us, the muscles we build at the gym are not for display purposes but for important functions like staying alive, maintaining health, or simply keeping our balance on unstable ground. Even though what we do at the gym is seldom duplicated in everyday life, the training is transferable … if I can lift a 50-pound free weight, I can figure out how to move a 50-pound sack of potatoes … if I can skip rope, I can climb stairs….

That's what happened to our friend Paul. Paul and his wife participate in 3Practice Circles. Much of the time, they run a trekking business in Asia; they return to the States periodically for family events. At their most recent Thanksgiving gathering, as families are wont to do at holidays, Paul's father and sister began talking politics. Dad is conservative, his daughter is liberal. When Paul heard their voices ramping up in the next room, he stepped in to intervene. Having been pushed during his 3Practice Circle workouts, now — when life presented the opportunity — Paul was able to referee for his loved ones, guiding them through simple 3Practice exercises that helped to remind them why they love each other even when they disagree.

When a person is ready, without notice, to engage at that level, that's relational fitness.

Inoculated

My wife Barbara and I were invited to dinner with two couples we've known and loved for decades. The women's civil behavior was never in question. The men's… well, that's another story.

Our friend Fred was already a 3Practice Circle veteran. Fred is quite conservative.

Our friend Jake had never been to a 3Practice Circle. Jake is very liberal.[25]

The meal was going fine. We were bantering about sports, sharing news about our kids and retelling favorite stories from our past together when, out of nowhere, Jake decided to share his feelings about the current occupant of the White House.

Apparently, Jake had forgotten about Fred's very conservative views and, oh-by-the-way, that we were sitting in Fred's house, at Fred's table, eating Fred's food. Jake carried on as if he were at a Bernie Sanders fundraiser: "Can you believe what that guy in the White House is doing? What a clown!" and so on… *Awkward* doesn't begin to capture the moment.

My eyes were glued on Fred. Waiting to see if he would do what I'd seen him do a hundred times before when he and

---

[25] Just so you know, I decided to change Fred's and Jake's names to preserve their privacy.

I got into this exact kind of exchange. Fred has opinions. He's thought a lot about why he believes what he believes, and he knows what he thinks of people who disagree with him. I've never known Fred to be any more reluctant than Jake about sharing his views, invited or not.

As Jake continued airing his unsolicited liberal convictions, Fred smiled at me and winked. As you know, a well-timed wink is the picture that's worth a thousand words. Fred, who knows I've always been more likely to agree with Jake's politics than his, was signaling that he knew there was a bond between the two of us, and that Jake was not in on it.

Having been in 3Practice Circles together, Fred and I had experienced moments like this before. In fact, The 3Practice Circle feeds off this sort of dispute — not so we can resolve the dispute but so we can be trained in what to do when we get triggered in real life. True to his training, Fred engaged Jake with clarifying questions to understand how he reached his point of view … Fred decided to stay in the room with difference … he decided against trying to win the point by comparing his best with Jake's worst.

Why did we design the 3Practice Circle this way? Because, in the same way that Jake launched into an unanticipated political rant, in normal life, awkward topics rarely announce themselves or ask permission. They pounce without warning, triggering reactions that can be surprisingly emotional, and at times overwhelming.

Our development process tackled the question: Can we train people for these unexpected moments? Can we prepare people to respond the way my very conservative friend, Fred, responded to our very liberal friend, Jake?

Needing to patch things up with a young relative during a vitriolic national election, gave my wife Barbara a new insight that led her to start referring to the 3Practices as *an inoculation against reactivity*. Here's what Barbara was noticing as a result of practicing the Practices in controlled 3Practice Circles:

We experienced newfound strength to resist the bait people dangled to lure us into fruitless arguing.

> We discovered that we had more empathy for the other than before.
>
> We found we were having more fun asking great questions than making great arguments.
>
> We learned that most folks with whom we have profound differences are disagreeable in very specific ways, but almost never in every possible way.

In a word, we'd been *inoculated* by our 3Practice Circle experiences. Here's a medical description of inoculation:

> Inoculation is "the introduction of an antigenic substance or vaccine into the body to produce immunity to a specific disease"[26]

---

[26] The American Heritage Stedman's Medical Dictionary, (Houghton Mifflin Company, 2002, 2001, 1995), cited by dictionary.com (https://www.dictionary.com/browse/inoculation).

The 3Practice Circle is a controlled environment where people are exposed through a dispute to just enough of *the difference disease* to provide emotional immunity, so that when they encounter the disease in an uncontrolled environment (a.k.a. normal life) they don't overreact the way my wife once did with our young relative.

You'll read more about the key elements in the 3Practice Circle shortly, but be forewarned: There's no guarantee the 3Practice Circle is for everybody. For some folks — a bit like receiving a physical inoculation — the initial side effects can be disturbing. The fact is, some people are just not ready to be exposed to what their ideological opposites really think. There's nothing quite as sobering as hearing your ideological opponent articulate a view that you think is not only wrong but possibly even dangerous, with the same tone of certainty you use when expressing your opinion. It's like that old saying, "You will know the truth and the truth will make you flinch before it sets you free."[27]

What happened at that dinner with Fred, my old friend, and ideological opposite, exposed us both for the umpteenth time to what we regard as the spread of toxic ideas from the other side. I think Fred is wrong and Fred thinks I'm wrong. I don't like seeing my country infected by Fred's ideas ... and he feels the same about me. What Fred and I do agree on is that we don't see that changing anytime soon.

---

[27] This saying is convincingly, if not definitively, attributed to Carlyle Marney, whose bio you can find at the Texas State Historical Association (https://tshaonline.org/handbook/online/articles/fmabm).

In spite of all that, we've decided that sharing a meal from time to time probably won't kill us.

We decided to take the risk and, so far, our inoculation against reactivity is holding up.

CH 10 | The Uncle Bob Moment

"We do not remember days, we remember moments"
— Cesare Pavese

True confession: Everyday potholes and bumps in the road sometimes throw me off stride. Annoyances as humdrum as my cell phone not working properly, or my car not starting, or getting pulled over for a penny-ante traffic stop can bring my blood to a boil. And I haven't even mentioned misplaced keys!

Thankfully, Silicon Valley recognized this as a market opportunity and rode to the rescue with a little product called TILE.

Tile is a two-inch square sandwich of plastic with something magical stuffed inside and a large button centrally located on the outside. When you push this button it "rings" whatever is wirelessly connected to it, such as your missing keys. Can you see why I appreciate this product?

Using Tile to locate misplaced keys is the very definition of utility — about as obvious as showing someone how to turn a page in a book or peel an orange.

Utility is what we were going for when we set out to design the 3 Practice Circles.

> We wanted to design a button we can push when someone pushes our button.
>
> We wanted to design a tool for people who didn't just lose their keys… they lost *it*!
>
> We wanted to create a product people could fall back on like a safety net when an *Uncle Bob Moment* catches them off guard and pushes them to the edge.

Uncle Bob[28]… Uncle Bob is anyone who knows how to push your button. There's a good chance that Uncle Bob is familiar to you, but sometimes he shows up disguised as someone you know barely or not at all. The worst Uncle Bob Moments occur without warning. You don't see them coming, which really pushes your button. It could happen at a family gathering, a workplace party, on the sidelines at a kids' sporting event, or visiting in the parking lot at your house of worship…. Uncle Bob could

---

[28] Apologies to members of the Bob Club [thebobclub.com]. I chose Bob, but it could just as well have been Tom, Dick or Harriet … or, you know, Jim.

turn up anywhere, at any time, to challenge you about anything:

"Hey, what's up with you ☐ supporting ☐ not supporting impeaching the president?"

"Hey, what's up with you ☐ agreeing ☐ disagreeing with climate-change legislation?"

"Hey, what's up with you ☐ praising ☐ condemning #metoo … #MAGA … #BlackLivesMatter"….

When Uncle Bob shows up — whoever he/she/they may be — you will be triggered.

trig·ger
noun

- an event or circumstance that is the cause of a particular action, process, or situation verb

cause (an event or situation) to happen or exist

(especially of something read, seen, or heard) distress (someone), typically as a result of arousing feelings or memories associated with a particular traumatic experience

— New Oxford American Dictionary

Here are symptoms of being triggered:

Feeling overwhelmed

A racing heart (a.k.a. flooding)

Anger

Acute sadness

Imagine telling Uncle Bob how much he offended you, dishonored your beliefs, or sounded like a bigot, without being accused of spoiling the meal? I know… not happening, right?

What defense do we have when people either a) don't know or b) don't care that they push our buttons … or, worse, what if they actually enjoy pushing our buttons? What are our options then?

And to complicate things even further, what if these are people we a) don't want to break up with (family and friends) or b) can't afford to break up with (bosses, co-workers or other nations)?

Here's how most of us have been conditioned to react:

> We avoid "them"
>
> We *trigger-shame* them by pointing out their insensitivity to our invisible pain
>
> We yell obscenities at them for offending us
>
> We say nothing in person and then jump on social media to belittle people like "them"

Finding an answer to the Uncle Bob Moment is what ultimately convinced us that merely teaching the 3 Practices or screening the *No Joke* documentary wouldn't be enough to move the needle on the problem of polarization. Tackling the Uncle Bob Moment forced us to gather actual ideological opponents in a room where we could test our hypothesis and develop our product. Remember, our customers told us what people wanted. It wasn't more inspiration or even that much new information. What they really wanted was for us to provide instruction and training — they wanted us to provide a place, a studio, a gathering where they could practice playing with the band.

That's what compelled us to create the 3 Practice Circle.

We started with a small circle, and as more people started showing up, we saw the need for rules to keep things focused and on track. That's how we came to draw on our experiences with learning communities, experiential learning design, board games, basketball, and music. We realized that the first, extremely practical, utility of the 3 Practice Circle was preparing people for their Uncle Bob Moments.[29]

We engineered backward and organized our entire product development process around finding the answer to just one question: *Where's the button I can push when somebody pushes my button?*

We knew that if we could help people solve their Uncle Bob Moments, many other important problems might be solved as a result. That's why this book is not a treatise on the 3 Practices but a handbook on the 3 Practice Circle.

---

[29] We've come to believe there's much more to it than that, but still … if all we accomplished was helping people learn how to not lose it when Uncle Bob pushes their button, that seems like a useful contribution.

You may have the best of intentions … you may want to make the world a better place … you may want to save the whales and the coal miners … you may be highly educated, well-read, and self-disciplined … you may believe in the dignity of every human, in turning the other cheek, in loving your neighbor as yourself … but when Uncle Bob (whom you love and definitely don't want to "break up" with) pushes your button, and all your good intentions become pavers on the road to hell, what will you do? What will you do?

Because, along with death and taxes, one more thing is certain: An Uncle Bob Moment with your name on it is waiting for you at an upcoming family gathering, a workplace water cooler, or a high school class discussion.

Imagine this. What if, when your next Uncle Bob Moment arrives, you could not only survive but actually flourish? What if you could out-listen Uncle Bob, stay in the room with him in spite of your differences, and resist the temptation to compare your best arguments with Uncle Bob's flimsy worst ones? What if you could translate your good intentions into dependable practices that have the potential to launch both you and Uncle Bob into a completely new kind of relationship — a relationship where the struggle to find agreement is replaced with a genuine desire to understand each other?

How do you develop the emotional and mental muscle memory that will keep you from treating Uncle Bob the way he treated you?

In a word … *practice*.

Chapter 11 | The Salt Shaker

When it rains it pours — Morton Salt Company

There's a story behind the Morton Salt slogan.

Just about forever, humans have been scraping, chipping, digging, evaporating, collecting, transporting, storing, distributing, and dispensing salt — moving it from where it occurs naturally to where salt is useful for preservation and seasoning. In the timeline of salt consumption, the common salt shaker, now as recognizable as a light switch, is late-breaking news.[30]

The simple reason for this is that, until recently, salt shakers didn't work very well… because, in the presence

---

[30] In fact, if you've traveled out where the streets have no names, you know there are people who have yet to see a light switch who know very well how salt shakers work.

of even trace levels of humidity — a common condition anywhere food is prepared — salt clumps and hardens.

Sure, people made salt shakers ... folks just didn't buy them, at least not for routine kitchen use. The first US salt shaker patent was awarded in 1858, to John Mason of Mason Jar fame. His glass shaker included a screw-on cap, naturally, with holes in the lid. The holes let moisture in, which made it difficult to let salt out. In 1871, C.P. Crossman's patent included an agitator to break up the clumps. That, too, failed to catch on.

Eventually, salt shakers were treated more like household knickknacks. A hollow replica of the Eiffel Tower with a couple of holes at the top and a plug in the bottom was novel, but no one thought of it as a reliable way to salt their eggs.

In 1911, the Morton Salt Company changed that for good — by changing salt not salt shakers.

The scientists at Morton figured out that adding a small amount of carbonate magnesium stopped salt from clumping and caking, without affecting the taste. The reboot was called *Morton's Free Running Salt*: "Morton's Free Running Salt Never Cakes or Hardens ... It Pours."[31]

Three years later, an advertising campaign introduced the Morton Salt Girl along with one of the stickiest slogans this side of *Jesus Saves*: Morton Salt ... *When It Rains it Pours*.

---

[31] "Her Debut," Morton Salt, (https://www.mortonsalt.com/heritage-era/her-first-appearance/).

With that advance, after just a few years, the salt shaker was elevated from novelty to ubiquity by utility — it just worked. And people across much of the world stopped caring where salt came from since, as everyone knew, salt came from salt shakers.

When you look at the travels, travails, and ultimate triumph of salt shakers, it's easy to conclude that utility is the first step on the road to ubiquity.

Morton got the salt part right — that's utility — and folks learned that nothing is better suited for seasoning to-taste than the wide-at-the-bottom, narrow-at-the-top, clear glass, screw-top container with the perforated metal lid — that's also utility.

There are more than a thousand patents on salt shakers, but really, who cares? After more than a century, the salt we shake in fancy restaurants, greasy spoon diners and home kitchens still pours from some recognizable version of that plain and simple salt shaker that just works. That's ubiquity.

Utility is the problem we're tackling with 3 Practice Circles. People talk all the time — like salt, there's no shortage of words. What's in short supply is clarity and understanding.

Expecting words to automatically convey understanding is a bit like standing outdoors, raising an electric lamp high in the air, and expecting the wind to light it up. There's a middle step — a purpose-built mechanism for converting wind to the electrical current that turns on the light. In researching, designing, testing, and refining 3Practice Circles, we've been working on a mechanism that generates clarity and leads to understanding when people listen to each other.

We're not the only ones working on this problem. In the face of our epidemic of polarization, a cottage industry of "dialogue" groups has sprung up across the nation.

"Dialogue" is in quote marks here because people use that word to mean different things. The best kind of dialogue takes time and a grasp of social dynamics that many of us haven't learned. This isn't bad, it's just not enough. It won't scale, which is why we've taken a different path in designing 3Practice Circles.

We want to reiterate that 3Practice Circles are not focused on creating thoughtful conversations or meaningful discussions. Neither are 3Practice Circles policy debates, panels, book clubs, encounter groups or sharing sessions. No, 3Practice Circles are something else entirely. Our product functions more like a game — a listening game where, instead of great ideas, cogent arguments, or sparkling exchanges, great questions become the winners.

Of course we want people to talk with each other and that is exactly what happens following a 3Practice Circle. After open 3Practice Circles, we just about have to kick people out so the person with the keys can lock up and go home. Every so often, two people who first met in a 3Practice Circle will include in their thank-you at the end that, to their mutual surprise, they've become friends ... they still don't agree about much, but they like each other, and when people like each other the rules change. Still, meaningful conversation is not our focus ... it's a byproduct.

Like conversation, agreement is a great idea. I wish we could all get together and agree on a few basics like truth, facts, gun safety, and tackling climate change.

However — not to beat a dead horse, but we'll say it again — *agreement is overrated* ... especially if by *agreement* you mean *100% alignment*, which is a notion with almost no potential for wide distribution.

Rather than agreement, we designed 3 Practice Circles as a distribution system for *understanding* — which is something almost everyone wants and almost no one knows how to get. Here's how we get to understanding in 3 Practice Circles:

> We think of the 3 Practice Circle as the salt shaker and *understanding* as the salt
>
> The special additive necessary to make the salt flow is *clarity*
>
> Clarity is the result of *disciplined curiosity*
>
> Disciplined curiosity is practiced through the act of asking *Clarifying Questions* which begin with a simple five-word phrase, "I'd be curious to know..."

When we say we help people learn three Practices and one Skill, the Skill is mastering the art of asking excellent Clarifying Questions … more on this shortly.

Chapter 12 | Setting the Table

In the present moment, when it comes to talking about politics, religion, gender, sexuality, power, ethnicity, history, economics, morality, life, the universe, and everything… many people find it difficult to act like adults.

Meaning: By and large, people do not play well with others.

Admittedly, none of us displays maturity a hundred percent of the time, but it's become difficult even to find people who understand that traits such as speaking and listening carefully and respectfully — waiting our turn, not interrupting or talking over others, steering clear of exaggeration, and not trying to impose our will on others — were once viewed as benchmarks of maturity to which we all collectively aspired.

Given that lack, we decided to test whether injecting a few simple rules into the process would enable 3Practice Circles to offset what's been lost in the adult conversational arts.

As a result of that testing, we identified five components that make a Circle work. This chapter explores two components that set up how the game is played. The next chapter unpacks three components that regulate how the game is played.

Framing the Dispute
3Practice Circles feed off differences that are genuinely disputed. If there's no dispute, it's just a friendly gathering. We purposely select Framing Questions that elevate issues people passionately disagree about.

The dispute can be broadly public, like climate change, water rights, or equal protection under law … or intimately personal, like gender identity, sexual attraction, or a woman's agency regarding her reproductive health.

The disputed topic doesn't matter as long as the Framing Question meets two criteria:

> first, it has to light up people who have something at stake

> second, it can't telegraph a preferred point of view — it must signal fairness to all comers.

Publishing the Framing Question in social media, emails, printed flyers, and personal invitations can attract people to upcoming 3Practice Circles.

We know a Framing Question is working when everyone in the Circle feels uncomfortable… but for different reasons. An effective Framing Question sets up a good emotional workout. The emotions are real — the relative safety of the 3Practice Circle makes them less intense than when an Uncle Bob Moment presents itself at a time and place of Uncle Bob's choosing.

Here are examples of good Framing Questions and why they work.

> **Are we on the Brink of Disaster or Halfway across the Bridge to a Better America?**
> A clear question anyone can answer from their point of view
>
> **Who Owns The American Story?**
> Crafted by an American Muslim as a way to talk about immigration
>
> **Judge Kavanaugh vs. Dr. Ford… Who Did You Believe?**
> Uses public figures as symbols of an age-old and universal controversy
>
> **What is Our Obligation to Fellow Americans Who Can't Afford Adequate Housing?**
> We learned that *homelessness* was too abstract for homeowners living in generally affluent communities but *affordability* did the trick
>
> **Is Racism as American as Apple Pie?**
> Links a warm memory with a shocking notion

Like bees to nectar, good Framing Questions attract ideological opponents to gather in a 3Practice Circle and look each other in the eye. Then we light a match and run… just kidding, we don't run.

Ideological opposites sit face to face in a 3Practice Circle because face time beats Facebook every day. Things change when we look into the eyes of someone we passionately disagree with. Things change when we sense the pain or hear the loss in their voice. Things get real when we watch someone stay in the room with people we know they passionately disagree with. The Framing Question sets the stage for all that. A good Framing Question works like that sticky melodic hook in a song we can't get out of our head, or what's commonly called an earworm.

The Head Referee
Whenever you and I join a group, we like to know the rules... Who has the power and what can we expect them to do with that power? That's why careful thought went into deciding what to call the person who's lent the privilege of guiding a 3Practice Circle.

For example, the title *Facilitator* might lead people to expect Circle leaders to make the process easier, while calling them the *Moderator* could signal that group safety and equal opportunity are priorities.

Since we have no control over who's going to speak up in a 3Practice Circle — no one has to say anything, after all — we can't promise that everyone will be heard. What we do make explicit is that anyone who talks will get a fair hearing.

Similarly, given the fact that the Framing Question is designed to trigger emotions, we can't promise everyone will feel safe at all times. What we do promise is that we will challenge and curb any comment or innuendo that remotely approaches a personal attack.

We don't promise agreement, resolution, or happy endings. We promise an environment that fosters greater clarity and understanding between people who disagree. And we do promise that you will be much better prepared the next time Uncle Bob pushes your buttons.

All this is in the context of two things we haven't made explicit. First, in the decades before we met, Jim Hancock and I were paid to lead hundreds of groups, across many different contexts, for many different purposes ... which is to say we brought an uncommon — not unheard of but uncommon — level of experience to this endeavor. Second, after every 3Practice Circle to date, we've taken time for an after-action review. In the beginning, these postmortems often took an hour; today, they seldom go beyond a few minutes. We still do these assessments because we're still learning. In was in an after-action review that it became clear that our principle role in a 3Practice Circle is ensuring fair play.

It was a short step from that realization to identifying the Circle leader as the Head Referee.

For better or worse, almost everyone knows how referees function in competitive sports. Good referees don't care who's in the game ... don't care if contestants win, lose, or draw. A good Head Referee works at being just hands-on enough to make sure that play is fair and players are reasonably protected from injury.

Fair play here includes the obligation to be governed by the clock, to ask questions that express genuine curiosity, to refrain from interrupting an ideological opponent with eye-rolling, muttering, huffing, and puffing. The Head Ref playfully but firmly reminds people to live up to these obligations.

Whenever possible, we include an Assistant Referee to assist the Head Ref. At some points, the Assistant Ref — using a different metaphor — functions something like an Emcee. For example, the Assistant Ref might get the Circle started with a welcome and a (very) brief introduction to what's about to happen, and then throw it to the Head Referee. As the Circle plays out, the Assistant Ref is free to ask an occasional Clarifying Question … or, taking pains not to hijack the Circle, the Assistant Ref may gently call foul if they think the Head Ref missed that a question seems unfair — something like, "Excuse me, but that question feels like an ambush to me — would you be willing to ask it another way, using words that are more neutral?" In a 3Practice Fishbowl, the Assistant Referee can work with the larger audience, pitching them questions to discuss on what they're seeing and hearing in the Circle, and moderating talkback from audience members to people in the Circle.

Taking care not to interrupt someone who is speaking, the Assistant Ref may whisper an observation about something the Head Ref may have missed — e.g. if another volunteer takes two minutes, there won't be time for Thank-yous without running over the announced closing time, and are you OK with that? The Head Ref and

Assistant Ref are free to trade roles at any point, for a few minutes or for the rest of the session. In a 3Practice Fishbowl, the Assistant Referee definitely functions like an Emcee, directing interactions with the larger audience, pitching questions to them, and managing talkbacks and Clarifying Questions from the audience to people in the Circle.

It's possible that having functioned as a second set of eyes and ears, the Assistant Ref's most important contribution comes in the after-Circle assessment with the Head Ref, when two heads really are better than one.

For the record, it must be acknowledged that we give the Head Referee one other task that, strictly speaking, moves her outside the bounds of refereeing.

Just about every 3Practice Circle is a learning experience, so we ask the Ref to watch for teachable moments and interject appropriate directions and insights. For example:

> If someone asks a Clarifying Question that is clear and to the point, Refs can, as they see fit, affirm the clarity and directness of the question.

> If someone poses a good Clarifying Question but then, persists in re-explaining why the question matters, the Ref can and should say, "I think your question is clear; you don't need to explain yourself." Then, to the one about to answer: "Do you understand the question?" If not, the Head Referee should invite the questioner to re-ask the question, using as few words as possible.

If someone is struggling to find the Clarifying Question they mean to ask, the Head Ref can focus the questioner by asking what she most wants the other person to clarify or expand … or, if it appears that what the questioner really wants is to take their own two minutes, the Ref can offer to add them to the queue.

We recognize that this turns the Head Referee into something like those Player/Coaches in some sports who stop play on the practice field to offer insights to their teammates. We're OK with this because in the final analysis a 3Practice Circle is designed to be more like a practice field than a playoff game. Which is why, in the controlled environment of a 3Practice Circle, we often discover that the people we started out thinking of as competitors turn out to be collaborators — our teammates in pursuing clarity, understanding, and connection.

Chapter 13 | Playing the Game

If you landed in this chapter without reading the one before, you've broken no laws but it will help you to read that chapter as well.

Here are the 3 Practice Circle components that regulate how the game is played.

The Clock
Time doesn't care what we think or feel, it is a fierce and unrelenting adversary. So, adding the element of time to the 3 Practice Circle — making the clock a central part of the experience — focuses the mind of each person in the Circle, increasing the pressure on everyone to be clear when they talk and pay close attention when they listen.

Managing the clock makes the Head Referee's job concrete and indispensable.

This is the first instance in which we ask people in the Circle to abide by an admittedly unnatural set of rules. It's the first acknowledgment that we're all choosing to live with the privileges and obligations of a social contract.

The clock also makes a 3Practice Circle a bit more like a game than anything we experience in real life. In real life, most of us never enjoy the luxury of two uninterrupted minutes to make our case, followed by Clarifying Questions from people who are genuinely interested in understanding — knowing that, before long, the shoe will be on the other foot and we'll be listening for two uninterrupted minutes to an opponent's case, followed by *our* Clarifying Questions. As in all games, temporarily accepting an alternative set of rules is the price of admission to a 3Practice Circle, and it works here much as if this were a game.

The Head Ref is in charge of the clock, with the duty to keep everyone abreast of how much time remains for the volunteer who is speaking — two minutes to respond to the Framing Question, one minute to answer each Clarifying Question, and 20 seconds to ask a question.

The 3Practice Circle clock not only creates a sense of urgency, it also provides relief, if for no other reason than to rein in the whims of someone who loves the sound of his own voice. Plus, when someone expresses something I find distasteful, I watch the clock for reassurance that it will end soon.

Here's something interesting we discovered about listening to our own voices for two minutes… It turns out that, symbolically, humans have something in common with Microchiroptera bats — those are the small, fast ones that are — sorry — blind as bats, and that, similar to porpoises and radar operators, use ultrasonic echolocation to keep from crashing into things. Humans in social interactions do something like this when we project our words to discover who's out there listening (or not). What those people reflect back — what "bounces" off them — can help us to know where we stand and keep us from crashing into others. The expression, "people remember what *they* say not what *you* say," is about this sort of relational echolocation ... as is the old gag, "Sorry, I've talked enough about myself ... now you talk about me."

In a 3Practice Circle, when no one interrupts us, all we have to go on is the sound of our own voice. What's fascinating about that is how many people — not everyone, but most — soon realize they can get a hearing without needing to shout or overstate their case. We witness people working to be clearer, more honest and certainly less hostile. Also, people learn to get to the point, which makes two minutes more than enough time for most of us to make our point. In fact, most people finish in about 90 seconds. Of course, there are exceptions, which is why the buzzer always goes off after two minutes.

On those rare occasions when someone is cut off by the buzzer, an alert Circle participant might pose the Clarifying Question: "I'd be curious to know how you would wrap that up if you had another minute." Everyone laughs, and the volunteer generally finishes up in less than 20 seconds.

Clarifying Questions

People are often initially attracted to a 3Practice Circle by the freedom to state their opinion in the presence of those who passionately disagree with them. On top of that, they hear that many participants will double down on their listening by following up with something like, "I'd be curious to know more about why this issue is so important to you." That kind of attention can be pretty intoxicating, especially when it's coming from an ideological opponent.

But interestingly, that's not what keeps people coming back. It doesn't take long for new people to figure out what we call the "game inside the game," which is mastering the skill of asking a good Clarifying Question. In reality, the entire 3Practice Circle experience is focused on helping people develop this one skill in the context of the 3Practices. To be sure, there are people who come to test and refine their arguments with the aid of others who will ask questions that help them find the holes. But even those people quickly learn that 3Practice Circles reward good questions over compelling arguments. They typically get worn down by the goodwill and positive role models and start to play along.

Clarifying Questions are important because, when Uncle Bob pushes your button, you need an alternative to arguing, yelling, and belittling — you need that button you can push when Uncle Bob pushes your button. Why? Because, when it's button-pushing time, your sweet Uncle Bob won't care what you think, and nothing you can say will persuade him that you're right and he's wrong. Of course, you can walk away … of course you can cut him off and dismiss him…. But, remembering in that awkward moment that Uncle Bob represents someone you want and maybe even need to stay connected to, you'll probably be looking for a solution less drastic than taking your ball and going home.

This sort of conflict can be unsettling, but there's a little secret that makes the Uncle Bob scenario slightly less daunting.

Remember that *understanding* depends on *clarity* — which begs the question: *Does clarity depend on anything?* In pursuit of clarity between ideological opponents, we'd narrowed our focus to helping Circle participants learn to find good Clarifying Questions. Then, one night, we tested the addition of a simple phrase, that has not only become part of the 3Practice Circle canon — but also the primary skill people walk out the door with, and often put into practice the same day. We discovered that relational clarity *is* connected to something — an expression of unfeigned curiosity, conveyed by the little phrase, "I'd be curious to know."

This is how it looks in a 3Practice Circle…

After a volunteer has taken their two minutes, anyone in the group can ask a Clarifying Question which *does not* sound like "I can't believe you said that!" but *does* sound something like "I'd be curious to know more about how you arrived at your opinion."

Remember, the questioner has 20 seconds to *find the question* and the volunteer has 60 seconds to answer. If the questioner can't find the question in 20 seconds, the Ref will offer help. If the volunteer's answer exceeds the allotted time, the Referee will say "Thank you" — which, in 3Practice Circle talk, means: "Please stop."

We train 3Practice Circle participants to begin every Clarifying Question with "I'd be curious to know." It's required. We tested other phrases like "could you say more about…" or "help me understand how, why or what…" but none of them delivers the relational bang for the buck of "I'd be curious to know." It's also worth noting that forcing people to lead with "I'd be curious to know" pushes them to find a true Clarifying Question that lives up to the promise in both substance and tone.

And one more thing: What with timers, and deciding whether to risk saying what we really think about a touchy subject and having to listen to people who irritate us, there is a lot going on in a 3Practice Circle. Frankly, knowing that our Clarifying Questions have to begin with "I'd be curious to know" is just one less thing to think about.

It turns out this may also be true in those unplanned Uncle Bob Moments. If I've already decided my first words when Uncle Bob pushes my button will be "I'd be curious to know," then I've ruled out yelling, or crying, or storming out of the room, or manufacturing statistics on the spot, or biting my lip and saying nothing. If I don't have to waste a heartbeat sorting through those options, then I'm free to find a really good Clarifying Question, fueled by genuine curiosity, to help me clarify what Uncle Bob is getting at. "I'd be curious to know why you imagine that matters to me" ... "I'd be curious to know if there's a bigger agenda behind your question" ... "I'd be curious to see your source material — I'm not promising I'd read it, but I'd be curious to know where it came from" ... "I'd be curious to know what you believe it costs you to have me on the opposite side of this disagreement" ....

Try it yourself. The next time you interact with colleagues, your kids, friends or an ideological opponent you bump into in the wild, ask them a Clarifying Question and preface it with "I'd be curious to know." You'll simultaneously experience the challenge of finding the question while practicing the skill of offering unfeigned curiosity — which is the gift we give people when we ask a good question. Watch their eyes to discern whether or not they believe you. Because, while people love to hear that you're curious, life has taught them to be skeptical because, as you know from personal experience, most people don't keep their promise to listen.

Say Thank You
When the live event planner Priya Parker says, "...we found that rules created intimacy," and "The proper use of rules can help you get so much more out of a gathering because it can help temporarily change behavior,"[32] she speaks to one of the key convictions that informed the development of the 3Practice Circle: A few simple rules can open the door for experiences that would not otherwise happen.

---

32 Priya Parker, The Art of Gathering, (Penguin Random House, NY, 2018), 137, 143.

A delightful example of this is a final rule we came up with that everyone seems to enjoy: We conclude each 3Practice Circle by inviting people to say, "Thank you."

They thank someone they observed being unusually interested in others or staying in the room emotionally with someone they disagreed with, or deciding not to play *gotcha* when someone said something that didn't add up. We give everyone an opportunity to express affirmation *specifically*, by taking the trouble to let someone know we caught them doing the right thing.

We allot time to find the words that express admiration, respect, and gratitude. We wait in silence until someone finds the words they're looking for.

This is often the most moving part of a 3Practice Circle. This is where people report transformative moments and making relational connections with people who, in spite of their profound and unchanging disagreements, they are coming to understand, respect, and maybe even admire and love.

One thing I can't recall ever hearing someone say at the end of a 3Practice Circle is; "Wow, thanks. Now I realize how wrong I've been all these years. From now on I'll stop thinking the way I thought before coming here."

Sounds funny but it illustrates an important point. We don't need people to change their minds or beliefs in order to participate in a 3Practice Circle. We need them to be open to understanding the other. At the risk of sounding like a broken record, let me repeat it: We don't need agreement. What we need is for people to want to grow up before they grow old, and maybe warm up to the notion of loving their neighbor the way they want to be loved.

Here are some thank-yous we've heard:

> Thanks for what you said. I never thought about that, I'm going to have to think about it more.
>
> I'm not comfortable with this white privilege thing, BUT when you talked about it, you really made me think. Thank You.
>
> I have never been in a group where I felt heard before.
>
> You did a great job of not comparing your best with the other person's worst.
>
> I'm not really into the white privilege thing but, after listening to your story, you've made me think.
>
> Your ability to ask Clarifying Questions is inspiring and helpful.
>
> Thank you for listening to me … I'm not used to that.

These are the gifts we give our ideological opponents in a 3Practice Circle. But it's not all for them. It's also for us, because when someone we generally disagree with says or does something we appreciate, the exercise of noticing, giving credit, and saying *thanks* develops muscle memory we can draw on the next time we meet Uncle Bob.

Chapter 14 | Practicing the Practices

All of this may sound magical ... which, when it works, it is. Nevertheless, learning new practices and skills is not *magic* — it takes attention, repetition, and refinement. In 3Practice Circles we direct, ask, encourage, and cajole people to begin every Clarifying Question with that little phrase, "I'd be curious to know." This could hardly be simpler if it weren't so hard. Of course, the hard part, really, is finding the will and discipline to repeat the phrase until "I'd be curious to know" replaces older habitual comebacks like, "Oh, for the love!" and "That's the most ridiculous/ignorant/offensive thing I've ever heard!" and, of course, that universal marker of desperation, "No, YOU are!"

That's why people come back to 3Practice Circles over and over: They come to practice sitting with ideological opponents in 3Practice Circles because it's a workout. In the safety of a stripped-down relational gym, complete with spotters to keep everyone as safe as possible, we exercise muscles we'll all need to flex sooner or later in the real-world.

❖ ❖ ❖

Uncle Bob *became* Uncle Bob to you because of his unusual talent for getting inside your head and under your skin. He may not even know that he generates feelings of dread, anger, shame, threat, humiliation or danger, but you do because you feel your adrenaline spike, your dry-mouth, hyper-alertness, tunnel vision, and elevated blood pressure which may trigger impulses to flee or lash out, or hunker down. That's a serious case of Uncle Bob-itis

What if we could reverse that? Seriously — what if we could disrupt those relationship-wrecking moments? What if we could learn to reprogram our response to Uncle Bob by practicing ahead of time for his unexpected appearances? What if we could hack the story we tell ourselves about Uncle Bob with the simple phrase, "You know what Uncle Bob, I'd be curious to know…"?

That's what happens in the 3Practice Circle. We reimagine our ideological opponents by engaging with them up close — but with a Referee to keep things from going sideways. And in the safety of the Circle, as clarity and understanding materialize, we can choose to connect or protect — depending on what's warranted.

We practice the Practices in a Circle so that when we're not in the Circle we can draw on muscle memory to seek clarity and understanding instead of retreating in fear and revulsion.

That said, remember that, in the chapter called "Three Things the 3Practices Don't Do," we said that practicing the Practices doesn't require staying in the room with a bully, or being unusually interested in a raging narcissist, or drawing a false equivalence between words and actions that are not comparable. We really mean that, and we train 3Practice Circle Referees to be very serious about keeping people safe.[33]

There are times when it becomes impossible to engage with or remain neutral about an ideological opponent's abusive words, threats, or actions. We don't endorse staying in the room with people who mean you harm. This goes for Uncle Bob as surely as it goes for a stranger.

Not comparing your best with Uncle Bob's worst doesn't mean you shouldn't confront injustice if you see it. If Uncle Bob exhibits a pattern of taking pleasure from inflicting pain, then Uncle Bob is a jerk, or worse. Pushing your button is one thing; intentional abuse is another. If you come to believe Uncle Bob is manifestly abusive, wall him off so he can't inflict further damage on you or others in your sphere. Of course, his exile doesn't have to

---

[33] We don't intend to patronize anyone on this point. Only some of us are positioned to assume positive outcomes without needing to think about it. A Ref who benefits from abundant cultural privilege might not recognize when a situation becomes unsafe for someone with less privilege. We met Saida Bulhan through the brilliant Aneelah Afzali, who leads the American Muslim Empowerment Network at the Muslim Association of Puget Sound (www.mapsredmond.org/?s=aneelah+afzali). Saida notes that giving people equal time to speak in a Circle doesn't automatically make the ground level and, of course, she's right. Saida's observation harmonizes with our notion that, "...as clarity and understanding materialize, we can choose to connect or protect — depending on what's warranted." No one should rely solely on the Referee to keep the game safe.

be permanent, but it does have to be persuasive. Civility is the price of admission to civil discourse. It is your right and responsibility to insist that everyone pay real money for their ticket.

Crossing the difference divide doesn't require surrendering good faith beliefs, abandoning principled convictions — or even changing your mind. In fact the opposite is true. Owning your opinions, values, and beliefs — while doing your best to stay connected to your ideological opposite — is the shift 3Practice Circles are designed to facilitate.

The 3Practices aren't about finding agreement. They're about clarity, and understanding, and finding a way to behave like decent, mature human beings in the middle of our disagreements.

And, for what it's worth, in the heat of disagreement, mature people don't think that asking for do-overs when they see they've offended someone is the same as giving in … a sincere apology resets the conversation — it's not waving the white flag.

Chapter 15 | Running in Circles … But in a Good Way

We wrote this book for people who are sad, angry, and apprehensive about important relationships being sucked into the vortex of the difference divide. We wrote this book for people who aren't ready to accept this as our collective new normal, where we have no choice but to write off relationships that mean a great deal to us.

This really happened…

The quiet gentleman listens attentively but doesn't say anything during the 3Practice Circle. He is in his late 60s, part of a small contingent of conservative folk who came to find out if we will really give them the freedom to say what they think, which is maybe not a given for conservatives living as a subcultural minority in my open-minded city of Seattle.

Following the Circle, people hang around, some of them making a beeline for whoever they seem to have the least in common with. People tell us they find it refreshing to be in a space where they can actually talk in person with a real-life ideological opponent — an experience they never have online. Something about being face to face makes it all different.

I introduce myself and try to make small talk with the quiet gentleman. He isn't having it. In the afterglow of the 3Practice Circle, small talk is the last thing he wants. "My daughter-in-law won't let me see my grandkids," he blurts. "In fact, both of my daughters-in-law have told us they aren't comfortable having the kids come around … My wife is heartbroken."

He's tearing up.

"What's the issue?" I ask, fervently hoping I'm not opening up a can of worms…

"I voted for Trump," he says, "and I have some views that they apparently find alarming." My heart falls to my feet. My two grandsons are the apple of my eye. I'm personally drawn into this guy's story. I can feel some of the pain he's feeling. I tell him how sorry I am, and then listen. I don't know if there's another side to the story — I imagine there is — but this conservative grandpa is in front of me now, and I'm ready to hear his story. What else can I do?

> We want this conservative grandpa to see his grandkids. We want his daughters-in-law to have confidence that their children won't be unsafe with him.

> We want neighbors to talk with each other about how they want to govern their communities.
>
> We want police to talk with dark-skinned Americans about equal protection under the law.
>
> We want religious groups to show mercy and grace — to each other and everyone around them.

Americans are distancing themselves from loved ones, avoiding family gatherings, dropping out of religious congregations, parting ways over social norms, breaking up over politics. It doesn't have to be this way, but at the moment this is exactly how it is. And, if we don't do something to change direction, it's exactly how things will remain.

That said … today is not the worst day ever.

We've read a bit of history and we know this is not the first time the United States have been divided down the middle. Much of our ongoing division is rooted in unfinished business from the past — neither gone nor forgotten — and many of our fundamental institutions, from political parties to financial systems to religious denominations were hammered out on the anvil of division. We've pulled ourselves together to rise above partisanship before … not permanently, clearly, but repeatedly. And here's an idea: How about, while we attend to the work left undone in our past, we simultaneously think proactively about our future together.

❖ ❖ ❖

We can talk about the 3Practices all day long, but we've discovered the most effective introduction to all this is live 3Practice Circles, with real people, on any topics our hosts choose.

We say, "Circles" and "topics" — plural — because once people see three or four 3Practice Circles, they realize it's not a fluke ... that the process works — whoever is in the Circle, regardless of the topic.

For a smallish group — up to 20 or so — we lead a 3Practice Circle where everyone can be involved. No one is compelled to say anything ... we never "go around the Circle" or call people out ... but anyone may volunteer to take two minutes to address the Framing Question, and anyone may ask a Clarifying Question.

For larger groups — ranging from dozens to hundreds — we form Fishbowl Circles of six-to-eight people who interact with each other while being observed by the larger audience. Along the way, we ask audience members to grab a couple of partners and discuss the process, and we invite them to ask questions of people in the Fishbowl.

When we connect with people who want to pursue the benefits of 3Practice Circles where they live and work, we offer training on how to lead and sustain private, organizational, and community-based 3Practice Circles — this is square one in 3Practice Referee certification.[34]

---

[34] For details on 3Practice Training and Referee Certification, visit 3Practices.com

If you'd like to bring us to your community, conference, company … wherever … use the Contact Us form at 3Practices.com. We'll do everything we can to find a win/win for working together.

❖ ❖ ❖

A Final Word
One of the interesting things about salt shakers is that they have no opinion about the product they contain. They're agnostic.

Similarly, 3Practice Circles are agnostic about motives. What motivates someone to cross the difference divide (fear, necessity, curiosity, fairness … maybe even love) is less important than learning how to do it — repeatedly and on purpose. We've spent a lot of energy learning to create spaces where folks come to understand each other without being obliged to agree. We're convinced that anyone with a hunger for renewing and strengthening human connections can set the table for others who want that too.

We know we're not alone. Most of our neighbors say they believe we can do better.[35] But, like agreement, good intentions are overrated. We can do better only by doing better.

So let's do that. Let's do better.

---

[35] Remember the 2018 Hidden Tribes Report finding that: "77 percent of Americans believe our differences are not so great that we cannot come together." Hidden Tribes: A Study of America's Polarized Landscape, (More In Common, Version 1.0.3, 2018), 5.

When all is said and done, we — meaning Henderson and Hancock — are not interested in returning to a time when things only *seemed* more harmonious, mostly because so many voices were excluded. The world is complicated. We share space with people who may never agree with us on things that really matter. But this state of affairs is nothing new, is it.... We'll never see the future by staring in the rearview mirror. So how about creating a collaborative future with people of good will who have learned to disagree, loud and late into the night, without wishing each other dead or incapacitated?

If creating that sort of future sounds as important to you as it does to us, let's do it together.

— Jim Henderson + Jim Hancock

ABOUT THE AUTHORS

Jim Henderson and Jim Hancock are content designers and producers. Over the years, they've delivered hundreds of films and live learning events aimed at helping individuals and groups evaluate where they are and chart a path toward where they want to be.

They move comfortably between organizational settings, business forums, civic gatherings and institutions of higher learning. They've worked with executive leadership teams ... designed curricula and resources to prepare dozens of trainers to guide the learning path of thousands of participants (Picture 8,000 people spread across the Washington DC Convention Center, all in circles of eight, learning the same thing at the same time, in a high-involvement learning environment). 3Practice Circles are among the most intimate and engaging learning environments the two have worked on (3Practices.com).

In 2016, a mutual friend put the two in a room where they could work together.

Prior to that meeting, Jim Henderson's innovative work in crossing the difference divide was reported by the *Wall Street Journal*, and *USA Today*, and featured on *This American Life* with Ira Glass. Jim is a serial entrepreneur, a producer of films and live events, an organizational leadership coach, and the author of eight books (JimHendersonPresents.com).

Jim Hancock has contributed to well north of 300 short films to help leaders create safe spaces to talk about unsafe things. He's written a dozen books on teenage crisis intervention, parenting adolescents, and equipping teenage leaders. Jim delivers creative and production services, books, movies, and experience-based learning (thetinycompanycalledme.com).

Together, the two Jims deliver 3Practice Circle experiences and training for community leaders, civic organizations, schools, businesses, religious leaders, and universities.

ACKNOWLEDGMENTS

A remarkable company of friends have influenced, aided, assisted, and supported us in developing *3Practices for Crossing the Difference Divide*.

We thank them all, especially — Aneelah Afzali, Uday & Preet Bali, Allen Belton, Peter Block, Daniel Bogard, Brian Boyle, Saida Bulhan, Kurt Campbell, Theresa Crecelius, Pat Dodd, Jim Doty, Mathew Francis, Namita Grace, Susan Hancock, Anita Hellam, Barb Henderson, Leigh Henderson, Chou Her, Cara Highsmith, Andy Himes, Todd Hunter, Tezcan Inanlar, Marvin Jacobo, Angela Jungwirth, Wendy Kennedy, Michelle Lang, Bruce & Beverly Logue, Lee Lor, Pete & Kathy MacKintosh, Brian McLaren, Matthew Mensinger, Kamil Mufti, Jeff Nagel, Leng Nou, Pat Patrick, Paul, Faith & Benjamin Petry, Jim Powell, Bryan Prosser, Luanna Putney, Ross Rettig, Pam Rice, Dave & Sharon Richards, Sol Rivas, Mike Schindler, Maureen Burke Schuster, Michael Skinner, Jeff Smith, Rob & Merle Smith, Wendy Spencer, Brian Wardlaw, Lisa Wellington, Teresa Wippel, John Yarborough, and Wm. Paul Young.

Made in the USA
Columbia, SC
15 February 2020